Atlas of Cultural Features

Atlas of Cultural Features

by Benjamin F. Richason, Ph.D.

Chairman, Department of Geography

Carroll College

A study of man's imprint on the land

Maps reproduced from selected quadrangles created by U.S. Geological Survey, Department of the Interior, Washington, D.C.

Hubbard Press

A division of Hubbard Scientific Company

Book design by Don Walkoe

Printed in the United States of America

Library of Congress Catalog Card Number 72-138629
Standard Book Number 0-8331-1301-1

The photographs in this book were reproduced through the courtesy of the following services:

Airpix, Chicago, Illinois
p. 2

Agricultural Stabilization & Conservation Service
pp. 10, 12, 14, 16, 24, 26, 32, 34,
48, 52, 64, 66, 70, 72, 78

U.S. Geological Survey
pp. 18, 30, 36, 42, 56, 60,
62, 82, 84, 86, 88

Soil Conservation Service
pp. 38, 80

Marc Hurd Aerial Survey
pp. 44, 46

U.S. Forest Service
p. 68

National Ocean Survey
p. 76

Dr. Benjamin F. Richason
pp. 22, 54

Contents

Introduction

Impressions of man's activities are apparent in almost all parts of the earth, to such an extent that it is unlikely the reader has observed a landscape completely untouched by man.

The part of the landscape which has resulted from the works of man is called the *cultural landscape.* Although it is often referred to as distinct, the cultural landscape does not exist in isolation. The man-made features of an area have been superimposed upon the physical setting and they exist within the framework of it—in some places conforming to it, in others altering it and in some places destroying it. The real world is a continuous mosaic of landforms, water bodies, vegetation, soil, settlement patterns and other cultural features which are interwoven to form a picture that reveals patterns of similarities and differences, and at the same time illustrates the distinctiveness and personality of individual areas.

Because the landscape of the earth is both physical and cultural, its study and interpretation require the use of maps on which both physical and cultural features are shown. The United States Geological Survey maps are primarily intended to represent the physical landscape; cultural features, however, are also shown on them. The features shown in brown represent topographic elevations or depressions, whether these have been produced by nature or by man. For example, natural levees along rivers, mine tailings and depressions produced by mining operations as well as contour lines are shown in brown. Features shown in blue indicate water bodies. Even such man-made hydrographic features as artificial lakes and drainage or irrigation ditches appear in blue on United States Geological Survey maps. Other cultural features are shown in red and black; however, on the maps in this book only black is used to show cultural features other than those of a topographic or hydrographic nature.

Many cultural features are shown by *pictographs* on the maps. Pictographs are symbols which resemble the actual cultural features, for example, houses, barns, factories, schools, churches, cemeteries, oil and gas tanks, mine shafts, dams, bridges, railroads, roads and many other features, which can be seen and identified on the map legend on page 9.

As the reader observes these map symbols he has to imagine their appearance in reality. The transition from the symbol to reality can be made when cultural features are observed in the field or on photographs. In this book, aerial photographs accompany most of the maps to aid in the identification of cultural features and in the interpretation of cultural patterns.

The aerial photograph shows the surface of the earth as it really is, with all of the details of various physical and cultural features interwoven in the general landscape. On the aerial photograph, field patterns and farmsteads, transportation networks and urban configurations, forests and croplands, along with landforms, waterways and soil patterns are seen as interrelated parts of the land.

Although the aerial photograph gives a true picture of the surface of the earth, a map is also necessary for the complete identification of some cultural features. For example, it may be difficult to tell the use of a building on an aerial photograph, but when the feature is labeled on the map or identified in the legend, little guesswork remains.

Many features that do not have direct landscape expression, such as political boundaries or survey lines, can be observed only on the map. On the other hand, boundaries and survey lines may be observed indirectly on the aerial photograph because, in many cases, these imaginary lines have been responsible for some of the cultural patterns in the United States. The survey and boundary lines, for example, that can be seen on the maps served as a framework for establishing some farm boundaries, fields, roads and city plans.

The 36 pairs of maps and aerial photographs in this book have been divided into six major sections of man's impressions on the land: *Survey Impressions,*

Rural Settlement Impressions, Agricultural Impressions, Industrial Impressions, Transportation Impressions and *Urban Impressions*.

A map in one section, however, may illustrate cultural impressions which are found in other sections. It would be difficult to find a map that represented only one cultural impression because of the many interrelated activities of man. As a result, most cultural features are closely associated with each other. For example, where there is an urban settlement there are also transportation facilities and industrial developments; where there is agriculture there are also rural settlements and small agriculture-oriented industries and services. Therefore, most of the maps in this book illustrate more than one type of cultural impression.

On the other hand, various aspects of a single cultural impression may be illustrated on several maps. For example, the iron and steel industry is represented on maps that are found in three sections. The mining of iron ore is shown under *Industrial Impressions*, the shipping of iron ore under *Transportation Impressions*, and the manufacture of iron and steel under *Industrial Impressions* and *Urban Impressions*. The maps in this book, therefore, could have been classified in several ways; the classification that is used is merely one of the ways. Furthermore, the collection of maps in this book obviously does not include all cultural features that exist. It represents only those which are considered to be of the greatest importance.

Each map in the book is identified by its latitude and longitude and, if appropriate, by township and range. A scale appears on each map that aids in the interpretation of the cultural features and patterns.

The scales of the aerial photographs used in this book range from approximately 1:10,000 to 1:60,000. The scale of aerial photographs is determined by the altitude at which the plane was flown and the focal length of the camera lens that was used. The scale of aerial photographs is also a ratio of ground distance between two objects to photograph distance between the two corresponding images.

The text associated with each pair of maps and aerial photographs gives the history of the cultural patterns as well as the conditions which led to their development. Following the text is a list of inquiries designed to provoke thought and discussion as well as to aid in the interpretation of the cultural landscape patterns. Attention is also drawn to the physical features of the areas discussed. A list of related maps is included. When the maps in each group are studied together, the major aspects of a human activity evolve. The maps show that there are many aspects to the cultural environment, that each aspect is interrelated with many others, and that all of these aspects are related to the surface of the earth.

The complete quadrangle maps and the photographs may be purchased individually from the government. Maps of areas west of the Mississippi River can be ordered from the *Distribution Section, Geological Survey, Federal Center, Denver, Colorado 80225*. Maps covering areas east of the Mississippi River should be ordered from the *Distribution Section, Geological Survey, 1200 South Eads Street, Arlington, Virginia 22202*. Orders for both eastern and western maps may be sent to either address. The name of the map may be found from the index sheet for the state, which can be obtained free of charge from either address. The price of a standard topographic map is $0.50.

Aerial photographs can be ordered from several government agencies and commercial firms. In order to determine which agency or company holds the negatives for the photographs desired, a map entitled *Status of Aerial Photography* should be consulted. This map may be obtained free of charge from the *Map Information Office, Geological Survey, Washington, D.C. 20242*. Before ordering aerial photographs, the photograph number of the frame desired should be obtained from a photo index of the county in which the photograph was taken. In many cases several index sheets are needed for complete county coverage. Photo index sheets are priced at $2.00 per sheet.

Related Maps

SETTLEMENT

Lakeside
Superior, Wisconsin
Fond du Lac, Wisconsin
Gary, Indiana

Oceanside, Estuarine
Charleston, South Carolina
Ventura, California
Washington, District of Columbia

Of Spanish Origin
Abiquiu, New Mexico
Gila Butte, Arizona
Ventura, California

Industrial
Gary, Indiana
Pittsburgh, Pennsylvania
Berwyn, Illinois
Duisburg, West Germany
Kansas City, Missouri

On Major Transportation Routes
Cumberland, Maryland
Duncannon, Pennsylvania
East Portal, Colorado
Middlesboro, Kentucky
Kansas City, Missouri

Of Tourist Importance
Ventura, California
Charleston, South Carolina
Fond du Lac, Wisconsin
Washington, District of Columbia

TRANSPORTATION

Across Appalachian Barrier
Duncannon, Pennsylvania
Middlesboro, Kentucky
Cumberland, Maryland

Across Rocky Mountains
East Portal, Colorado

Across Great Plains
Scottsbluff, Nebraska

For Industrial Goods
Superior, Wisconsin } Water
Romeoville, Illinois. } Water / Railroad
Berwyn, Illinois } Railroad

INDUSTRY

Iron and Steel
Hibbing, Minnesota
Aurora, Minnesota
Superior, Wisconsin
Coal City, Illinois
Gary, Indiana
Duisburg, West Germany
Romeoville, Illinois
Berwyn, Illinois

Extractive
Bingham Canyon, Utah
Aurora, Minnesota
Hibbing, Minnesota
Coal City, Illinois
Keeler, California
Empire, Louisiana

RURAL SETTLEMENT

Riverside—Abiquiu, New Mexico
Beatrice, Nebraska

HAMLETS

Antioch, Nebraska
Bleecker, Alabama
Buckingham, Iowa
Fulton, Indiana

AGRICULTURE

Tropical
Arecibo, Puerto Rico
Hilo, Hawaii

Dryland
Abiquiu, New Mexico
Gila Butte, Arizona
Antioch, Nebraska

Commercial
Buckingham, Iowa
Antioch, Nebraska
Arecibo, Puerto Rico
Hilo, Hawaii
Gila Butte, Arizona

Subsistence
Bleecker, Alabama
Abiquiu, New Mexico

SURVEY

Origin
East Liverpool, North Ohio/
Pennsylvania/Virginia

Conformity to Survey Lines
Buckingham, Iowa
Beatrice, Nebraska

Digressions from Survey Lines
De Pere, Wisconsin
Empire, Louisiana
Fulton, Indiana
Anoka, Indiana

TOPOGRAPHIC MAP SYMBOLS

VARIATIONS WILL BE FOUND ON OLDER MAPS

ap Symbols

'd surface, heavy duty road, four or more lanes
d surface, heavy duty road, two or three lanes
'd surface, medium duty road, four or more lanes
d surface, medium duty road, two or three lanes
roved light duty road
mproved dirt road and trail
l highway, dividing strip 25 feet or less
l highway, dividing strip exceeding 25 feet
d under construction

road, single track and multiple track
roads in juxtaposition
row gage, single track and multiple track
road in street and carline
ge, road and railroad
wbridge, road and railroad
tbridge
nel, road and railroad
rpass and underpass
ortant small masonry or earth dam
ı with lock
ı with road
al with lock

dings (dwelling, place of employment, etc.)
ool, church, and cemetery — Cem
dings (barn, warehouse, etc.)
er transmission line
phone line, pipeline, etc. (labeled as to type)
s other than water (labeled as to type) — Oil, Gas
ks; oil, water, etc. (labeled as to type) — Water
ated or landmark object; windmill
n pit, mine, or quarry; prospect
ft and tunnel entrance

zontal and vertical control station:
'ablet, spirit level elevation — BM △5653
)ther recoverable mark, spirit level elevation — △5455
zontal control station: tablet, vertical angle elevation — VABM △9519
ny recoverable mark, vertical angle or checked elevation — △3775
ical control station: tablet, spirit level elevation — BM ×957
)ther recoverable mark, spirit level elevation — ×954
:ked spot elevation — ×4675
necked spot elevation and water elevation — ×5657 — 870

Boundary, national
State
County, parish, municipio
Civil township, precinct, town, barrio
Incorporated city, village, town, hamlet
Reservation, national or state
Small park, cemetery, airport, etc.
Land grant
Township or range line, United States land survey
Township or range line, approximate location
Section line, United States land survey
Section line, approximate location
Township line, not United States land survey
Section line, not United States land survey
Section corner, found and indicated
Boundary monument: land grant and other
United States mineral or location monument

Index contour
Intermediate contour
Supplementary contour
Depression contours
Fill
Cut
Levee
Levee with road
Mine dump
Wash
Tailings
Tailings pond
Strip mine
Distorted surface
Sand area
Gravel beach

Perennial streams
Intermittent streams
Elevated aqueduct
Aqueduct tunnel
Water well and spring
Disappearing stream
Small rapids
Small falls
Large rapids
Large falls
Intermittent lake
Dry lake
Foreshore flat
Rock or coral reef
Sounding, depth curve — 10
Piling or dolphin
Exposed wreck
Sunken wreck
Rock, bare or awash; dangerous to navigation

Marsh (swamp)
Submerged marsh
Wooded marsh
Mangrove
Woods or brushwood
Orchard
Vineyard
Scrub
Inundation area
Urban area

Survey Impressions

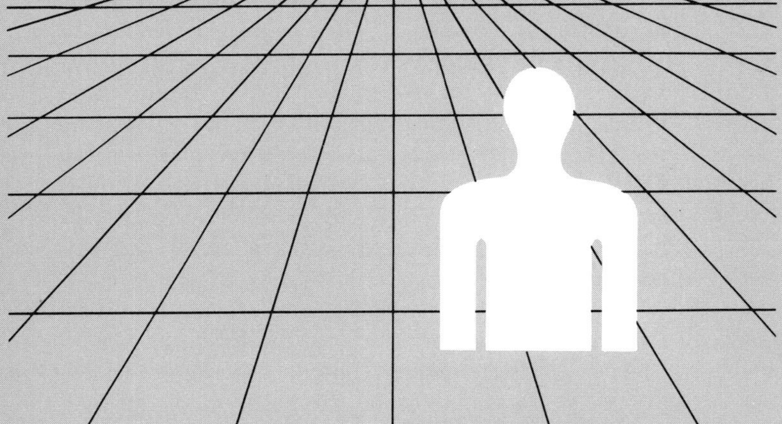

The pattern of cultural features in the major part of the United States reflects the survey system that was developed before the country could be settled. Following the Revolutionary War the new nation found itself deeply in debt, and, at the same time, in the real-estate business. If revenue was to be derived from the newly acquired lands in the west, they had to be sold and settled. Before the land could be sold, a system of land description had to be inaugurated so that ownership could be accurately recorded. Such a system was defined in the Land Ordinance of May 20, 1785. From this ordinance stems the basis of property ownership in many parts of the United States. The survey lines which were subsequently established influenced the pattern of settlement and the arrangement of cultural features on the land more than any other single event in United States history.

The Public Land Survey divided up the lands north and west of the Ohio River into squares (Townships) six miles on a side. Base lines were established and Township areas of six-mile widths were demarcated north and south of the lines. Principal meridians were established and Ranges were surveyed at six-mile intervals east and west from the meridians. The 36-square-mile area thus delimited is known as a Congressional Township. The Townships were eventually subdivided into Sections, one mile on a side.

The stage was set for the rectangular pattern of the American landscape. Land was sold in rectangular subdivisions of the Section. A 160-acre farm in the southeastern part of Section 10, T2N, R1E, for example, would be designated as the SE¼, Sec. 10. Field boundaries corresponded to the rectangular boundaries of the farm, and a field might be designated by the farmer as the "back forty," which would be one-quarter of a quarter section. Villages were laid out to conform to the survey lines. Roads followed the section and half-section lines, and dwellings were erected along the roads.

Some lands within the Township were designated for special purposes. There were the School Sections, Wagon Road lands and Canal lands; the monies from the sale of these lands were to be used for the building of schools, roads and canals, respectively.

Cultural features do not always coincide with the survey lines. In some parts of the country settlement predated the coming of the Deputy Surveyors. In areas of early French or Spanish settlement, of private land settlement schemes or of Indian land grants, boundary lines had been established by the time the United States surveyors arrived. Here, the Public Land Survey lines were discontinued in preference to the preceding cadastral lines, and, in many cases, modern field patterns, roads and settlements conform to the former settlement base.

Other examples of the nonconformity of cultural features to the survey lines can be found in rugged terrain. In these places topography gained precedence; settlements, roads and other cultural features were located in the most accessible areas.

The following maps have been selected to show survey line impressions. In themselves they are not part of the observable landscape. The indirect impressions of the survey lines, however, can be observed in terms of road and settlement patterns, along with townsite location and pattern. Churches, schools and cemeteries were characteristically located at section corners because of the intersections of the rectangular road patterns.

Reference to the aerial photographs will reveal the influence survey lines have had on field boundaries.

EAST LIVERPOOL NORTH, OHIO/PENNSYLVANIA/WEST VIRGINIA

The historic marker in the southeastern part of the map marks the beginning of the United States Public Land Survey. Actually, the marker is about 1,112 feet north of the point where the original survey was started. This point was the beginning of the survey of millions of acres of public domain north and west of the Ohio River. Once the lands were surveyed they could be identified, sold and settled. The survey was the first national cadastral survey, and it served as a model for similar surveys in other countries.

The Public Land Survey was authorized by the Ordinance of May 20, 1785. It stated that the public domain would be surveyed into townships of 36 square miles. A series of east-west lines and north-south lines were to be established six miles apart with reference to established base lines and principal meridians, thus dividing the land into 36-square-mile townships. The townships were to be subdivided into 36 square sections, one mile on a side. Therefore, each section contains 640 acres of land and a quarter section contains 160 acres.

The survey was begun on September 30, 1785, by Thomas Hutchins, the first geographer to the United States. He and his deputies hacked four miles of the first east-west base line within the following month. This line, and its subsequent extensions, became known as the Geographer's Line.

At the end of the first six miles of this line a north-south line was surveyed southward to the Ohio River to create the first township. Several such lines, six miles apart, were marked up to the Ohio River. The east-west areas between these lines are known as ranges.

1. Why is the marker north of the actual point it represents? Locate the actual point on the map. Why was this location chosen for the beginning of the survey?
2. On the map, find the first township to be surveyed.
3. Why do the road and settlement patterns not conform to the survey lines?
4. Is the Ohio River navigable in this area? Support your answer from evidence on the map and photograph.
5. What industries can you identify in this area?

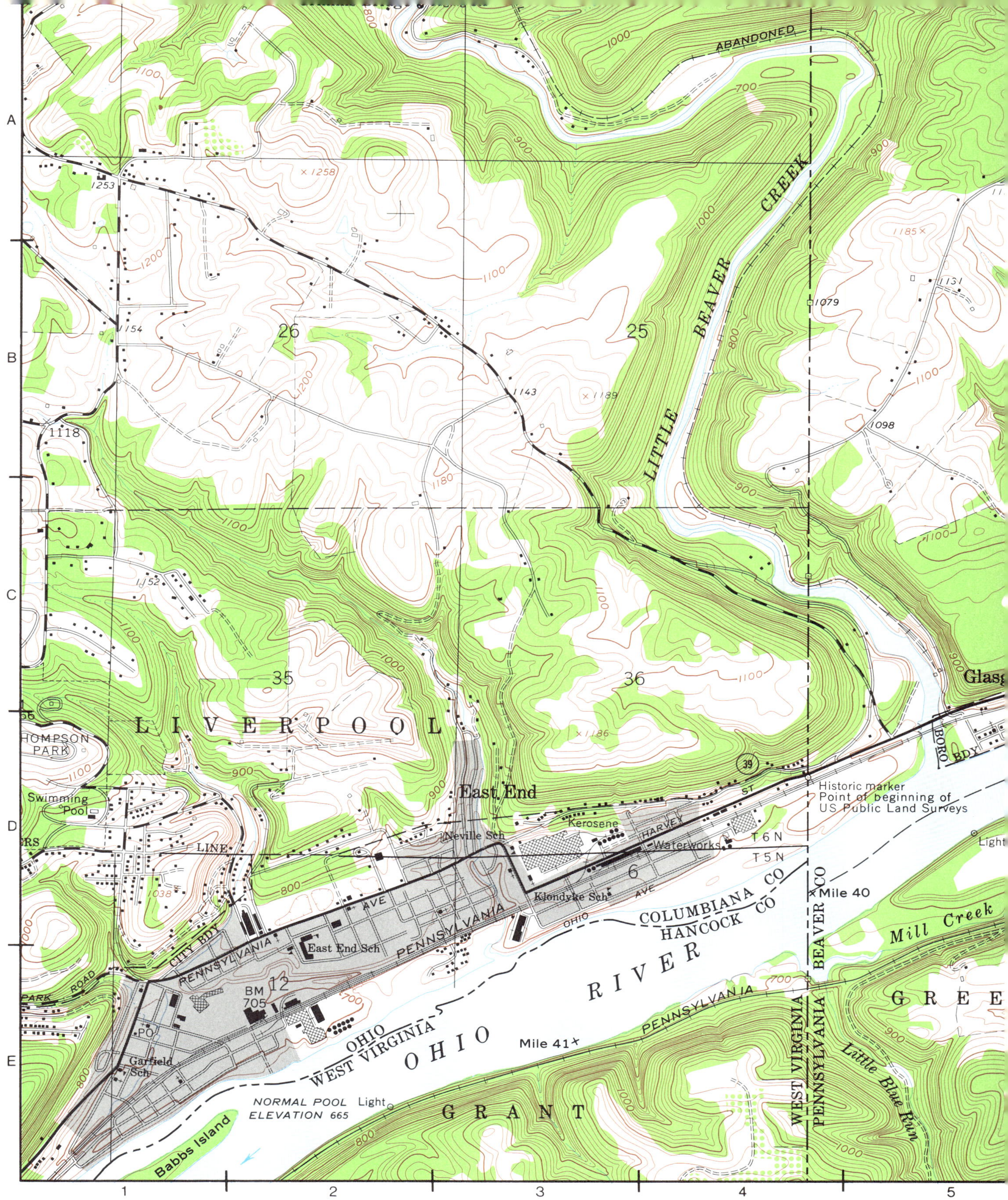

from East Liverpool North Quadrangle, Ohio/Pennsylvania/West Virginia

Scale 1:24,000
Contour Interval 20 ft.
Latitude 40° 37′ 30″ N to 40° 40′ 30″ N
Longitude 80° 31′ W to 80° 33′ 30″ W

FULTON, INDIANA

As the Public Land Survey extended westward, it encountered areas which had been surveyed previously. One such region can be seen on the map of Fulton, Indiana. A strip of land for the Michigan Road was obtained from the Pottawatomie Indians by the Treaty of October 16, 1826. This land already had been surveyed and divided in connection with the building of the road in 1828-1829, while the Public Land Survey was completed after 1830. Sections 40, 41 and 42, along the road form an echelon pattern instead of a grid.

The part of the Michigan Road shown on this map was opened between 1831 and 1837, but it remained impassable during much of the year. In 1831 the road was improved: all timber and underbrush were cleared leaving no stumps over one foot high, the creek banks were graded and the swamps causewayed. Thus, the road was made passable by wagons from Michigan City to Madison on the Ohio River, by way of South Bend, Logansport, Indianapolis and Greensburg.

The newer Public Land Survey did not conform to the previous sections, and partial sections remained where the two met. Since the field boundaries conform to the Survey lines of their respective areas, they are offset where the two areas meet. Some east-west roads that follow the Public Land Survey section lines make bends to continue along the Michigan Road section lines.

In 1831 lands bordering the road were sold. The smallest tract offered for sale was 80 acres or half of a quarter-section. The quarter sections adjacent to the road were divided in north-south halves, while the others were divided in east-west halves.

1. Why is the width of Section 35 not the same as the width of Section 42?
2. Why are there numerous ditches in this area?
3. In what physiographic section is this area located?
4. Describe the rural settlement pattern.
5. Account for the fact that much of the early Michigan Road was impassable during parts of the year.
6. Compare the rural farm population density in this area north of the Wabash River to that of the area south of the Wabash River on the Anoka quadrangle.

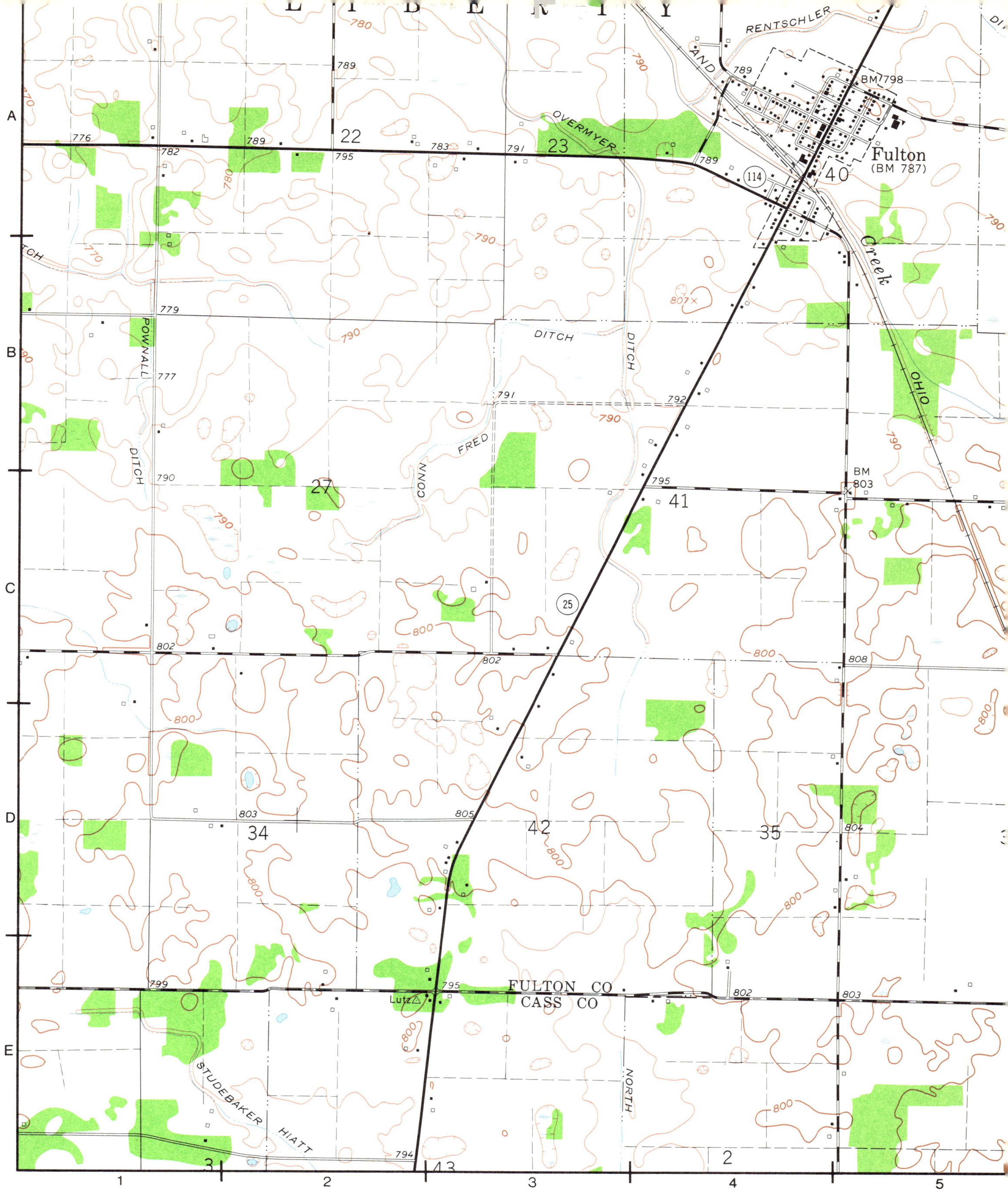

from Fulton Quadrangle, Indiana

Scale	1:24,000
Contour Interval	10 ft.
Latitude	40° 54′ N to 40° 57′ 30″ N
Longitude	86° 15′ W to 86° 18′ 30″ W

½ 0 1 MILE

1 .5 0 1 KILOMETER

ANOKA, INDIANA

The Public Land Survey System is interrupted in places by Indian land grants, which can be observed on the map, south of the Wabash River, on either side of Morgan Hill Road and south of Kienly Island. Their boundaries were delimited prior to the government surveys that were completed in late 1839 in this area.

Many of the Indians held their land for a number of years; however, some Indians sold their grants to European settlers shortly after the lands were obtained. The Indian Treaty Lands occupy the steep bluffs and gravel terraces along the Wabash River. These lands were in demand by the early settlers because the lands were located near a large, natural waterway and they were well drained. The areas along the Wabash River in between the reservations were the first to be purchased by the early settlers. South of the Wabash River bluffs, the land is a poorly drained till plain, which required numerous drainage ditches for crop production and the control of malaria. Roads tend to follow the section and half-section lines in this level country.

The leading crops are corn, oats, hay, wheat and soybeans. Dairy and beef cattle and swine are raised throughout the region. The major settlement, Logansport, was a division point on the Pennsylvania Railroad.

1. How are the boundaries of the Indian land grants shown on the map? How would land ownership be described in these areas today?
2. Where are rural dwellings situated in relation to the roads?
3. Estimate the rural farm population density south of the Wabash River.
4. What does the complex pattern of railroad tracks indicate? Account for the location of the railroads on the map.
5. What evidences can you see on the map and photograph that indicate the former wetness of the area south of the Wabash River?
6. What is a till plain? Account for the fact that most of the soils in the till plain are poorly to imperfectly drained.

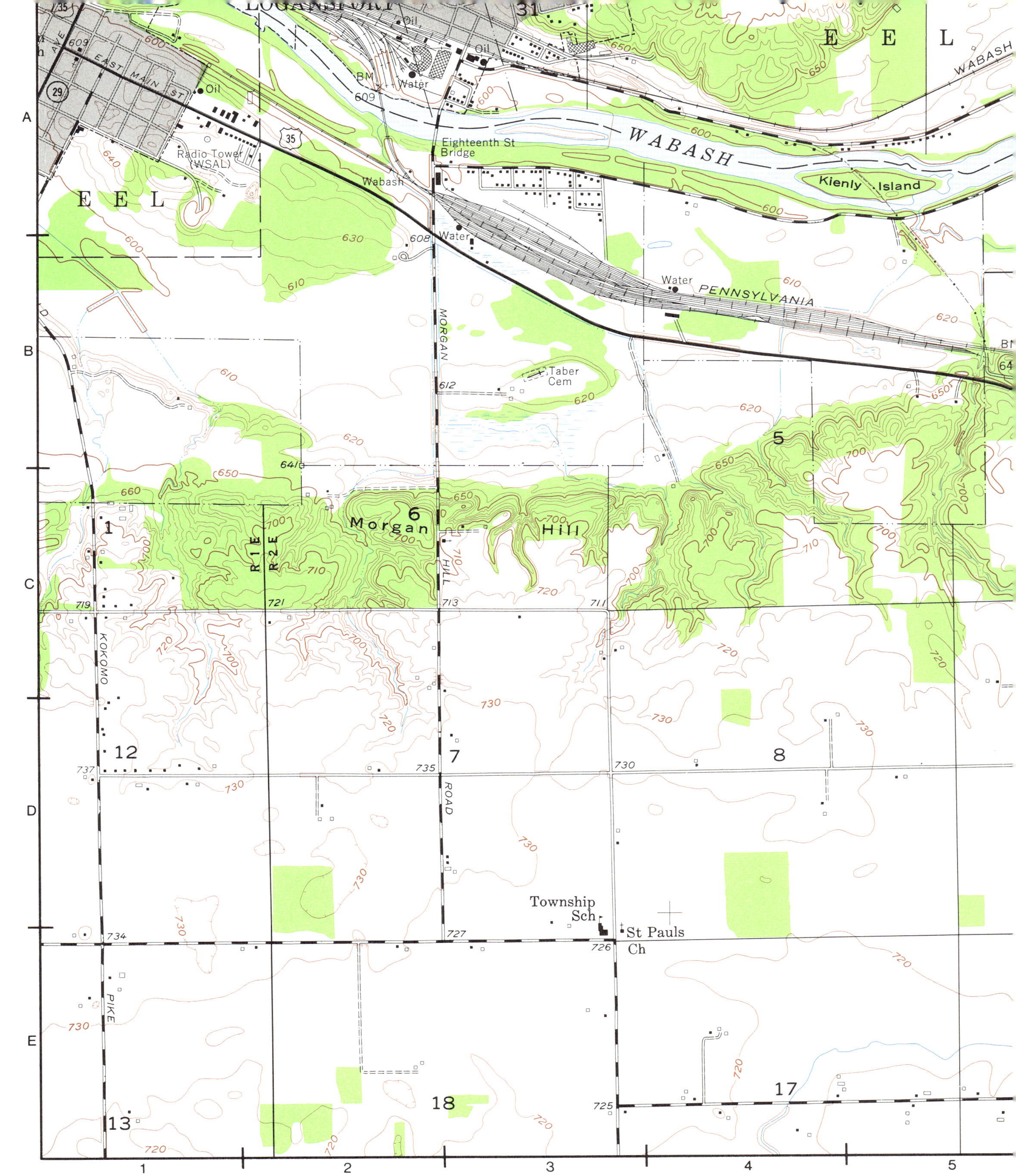

from Anoka Quadrangle, Indiana

Scale 1:24,000
Contour Interval 10 ft.
Latitude 40° 42′ N to 40° 45′ N
Longitude 86° 18′ 30″ W to 86° 22′ W

½ 0 1 MILE
1 .5 0 1 KILOMETER

DE PERE, WISCONSIN

The map and photograph show the French seigniorial system of land division near Green Bay, along the Fox River in Wisconsin. This region, one of the first to be settled in Wisconsin, was claimed for France by Jean Nicolet in 1634. The first settlement, the St. Francis Xavier Mission, was built by Father Claude Allouez in 1671. By 1684, French soldiers, traders, trappers and missionaries had begun to settle along the Fox River. Land along the river was highly prized; therefore, most landholdings had narrow river frontage and extended inland as long narrow strips. Ownership of these lands was identified by metes and bounds.

Following 1761 the region was occupied first by the British and then by the Americans. The French influence persisted until the War of 1812, after which Americans gained control.

When the Public Land Survey came to this area, the old seigniorial system was maintained and each holding was given a number. Green Bay, a part of which can be seen in the northeast corner of the map, and De Pere were platted between 1829 and 1835. The streets in De Pere and the roads of the surrounding countryside are strongly influenced by the land division system. The modern field patterns are also impressions of the old seigniorial survey.

The completion of the De Pere dam on the Fox River in 1849 introduced industry to De Pere. Mills engaged in grinding grain and sawing and processing wood sprang up. Even today the Fox River banks are highly industrialized.

1. Explain the orientation of country roads and city streets in this area.
2. Why was water frontage important for the French landholders? This area is located between the former French holdings in Canada and Louisiana. Does this suggest a reason for the early importance of the site?
3. What industries can you identify on the aerial photograph?
4. What are the major forms of transportation shown on the map? Explain their location.
5. Describe the field patterns as seen on the photograph. What crops can be identified in the fields?
6. How is land identified by metes and bounds? Give an illustration by using an actual example from the map.
7. What is the European origin of the seigniorial system of land subdivision?

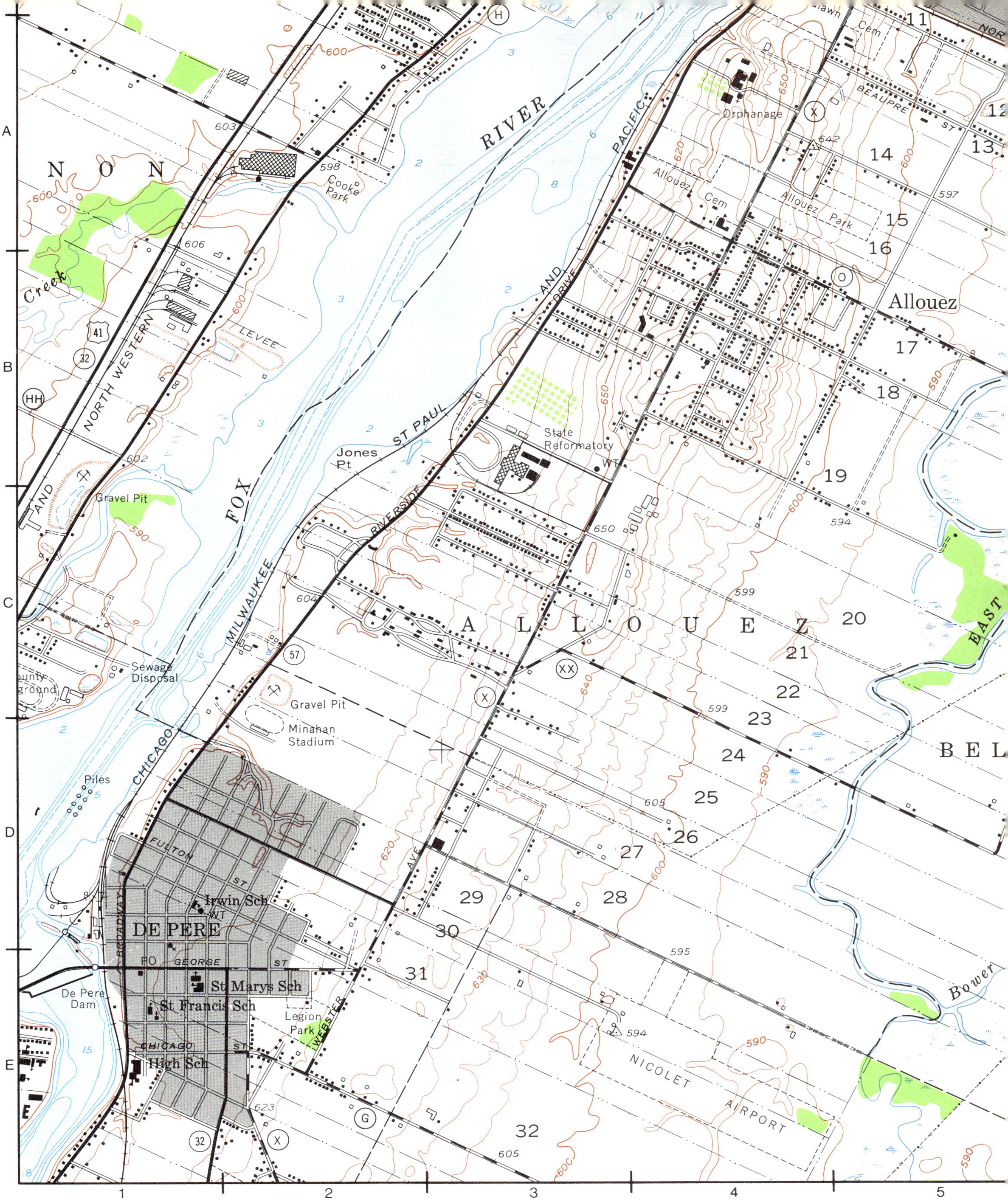

from De Pere Quadrangle, Wisconsin—Brown Co.

Scale	1:24,000
Contour Interval	10 ft.
Latitude	44° 26′ 33″ N to 44° 29′ 30″ N
Longitude	88° 00′ 30″ W to 88° 04′ W

½ 0 1 MILE

1 .5 0 1 KILOMETER

EMPIRE, LOUISIANA

The explorations of René Robert Cavelier, Sieur de la Salle, in 1682 opened the lower Mississippi delta to French settlers. In 1698, the Le Moyne brothers began colonizing the lower Mississippi River borderlands. The settlement patterns that resulted persist today. (See De Pere Quadrangle, Wisconsin).

The early settlements were limited to the natural levees. The well-drained sand and gravel levees, that rise 10 to 12 feet above the river, provided the only suitable sites for settlement. In addition, the levees were close to the river, which was the only means of transportation. Since water frontage was so important, land holdings assumed the shape of long narrow strips extending from the river into the back swamps. Recently when the township and range system of land survey was extended into the area, the old French land divisions were not disturbed and each division was given a number for ownership identification.

The cultural impressions on both the map and the photograph show the association of the levees and agriculture. Almost all settlements are found along the natural levees of the Mississippi River.

As the population increased and settlements grew, activities diversified. Fishing for shrimp, crab and oysters along with trapping muskrat for fur became important industries. The products supplied not only the local people, but also the markets of New Orleans to the north.

Further exploration and settlement led to the discovery and exploration of mineral wealth. The map shows evidence of sulphur, salt and petroleum. Pipelines from the offshore oil platforms can be seen on the map.

1. Are there any similarities between the land division systems of Empire, Louisiana, and De Pere, Wisconsin? Explain.
2. Where are the fields located with respect to topography? Why?
3. What are the signs of industrialization in the region?
4. Describe the pattern of settlement.
5. Why do the roads parallel the river?
6. How are natural levees formed? What is an artificial levee? Locate artificial levees on the map and photograph.
7. What is a back swamp?
8. The Acadians settled in this area in 1760. Who were they and why did they settle here?
9. What place names on the map are of French origin? What place names are not of French origin? Account for the latter.

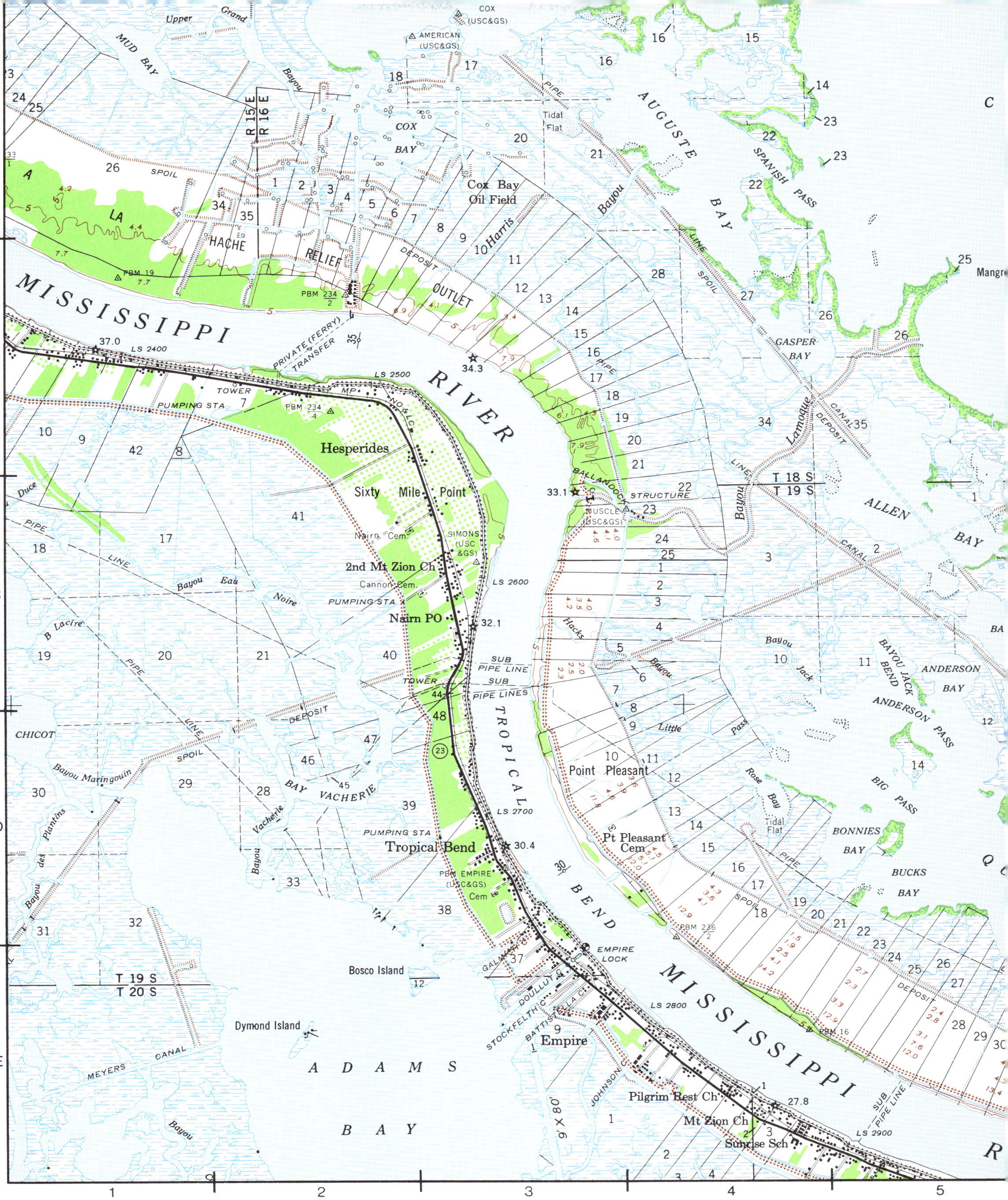

from Empire Quadrangle, Louisiana—Plaquemines Parish

Scale 1:62,500
Contour Interval 5 ft.
Latitude 29° 22′ N to 29° 30′ N
Longitude 89° 32′ W to 89° 40′ W

½ 0 1 2 3 4 MILES

1 .5 0 1 2 3 4 5 KILOMETERS

Rural Settlement Impressions

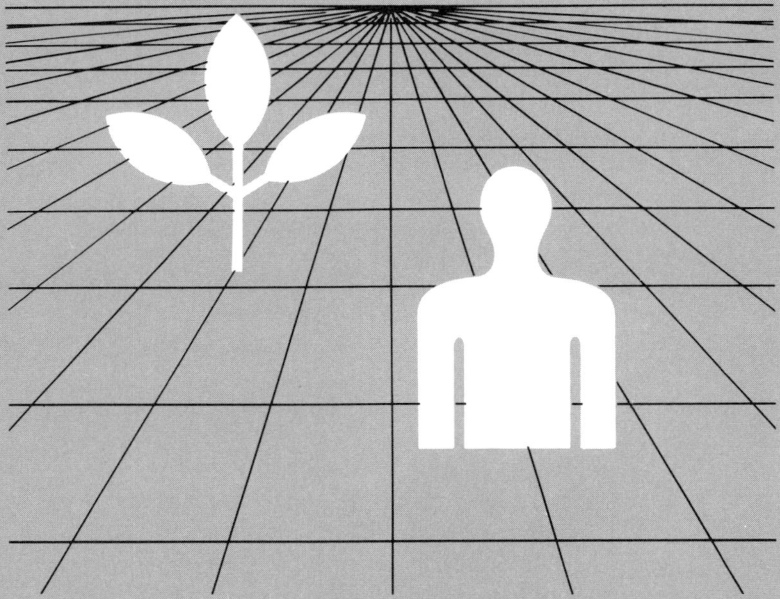

Prior to 1920, most of the population of the United States was rural. Initially, farmers produced just enough food for subsistence, but when transportation was improved and cities expanded, farm production became export oriented.

American farmers, unlike the farmers of most other parts of the world, have almost always lived on their farms. Proximity to a stream or river was essential for water supply and transportation, and on prairies the trees along the streams provided lumber for fuel and construction. Furthermore, the valleys were more fertile and provided level land, which once cleared, made the best cropland.

Settlement in the valleys proceeded even more rapidly when transportation routes were extended toward the interior. The routes usually followed the valleys because they provided the greatest ease of construction. The roads not only united existing communities but also brought more settlers to the valleys. When artificial drainage became possible, more of the poorly drained soils were brought under cultivation and settlement continued to expand.

Property boundaries followed the rectangular pattern of the Public Land Survey in the midwest. The farms, fields and road patterns that developed in conjunction with the property divisions also acquired a rectangular pattern. In the east and south, rural property boundaries followed older land division systems or natural features such as streams or valleys. Roads to the settlements were usually built along ridgetops or valleys. Subsequent settlement followed the roads, therefore, a linear pattern oriented to topography developed. Today, the rural landscape is traversed by multilane, limited access highways and railroads that follow the easiest routes. Dwellings and service structures cluster at points of access and interchanges. Rural dwellings, however, remain dependent on country roads.

The nature of the farmstead ranges from complex assemblages of milking barns, silos, bulk-tank storage and machine sheds of the Wisconsin dairy farm to the few simple structures of a central Illinois cash-grain farmstead. The plantations and ranches have structures that are entirely different.

Another element of rural settlement is the hamlet. Such settlements are shown on maps in the section on Agriculture. Most of the small population of the hamlet provides services to the surrounding agricultural region. The street pattern of the hamlet usually parallels the nearest road or railroad and is, therefore, not necessarily oriented in a north-south, east-west direction. The hamlet usually has a church with a burial ground, school, general store, filling station with a garage, an implement and feed store, restaurant and perhaps a bar. The proprietors of these services, together with some retired farmers, make up the principal population of the hamlet.

The following maps illustrate rural settlement patterns. In addition, many of the maps of other sections illustrate the relation of rural settlement to the survey system and agricultural practices.

BEATRICE WEST, NEBRASKA

Near the center of this map is the Homestead National Monument, which commemorates the free land policy that governed the settlement of the western plains. It marks the site of the first homestead to be established after the liberalization of the land laws.

In 1820, the federal government encouraged the settlement of the western territories by selling the lands at only $1.25 an acre. The minimum amount of land sold was 80 acres; therefore, a farm could be purchased for as little as $100. But few people could afford even $100, and many settlers simply "squatted" on the land and began to cultivate it without a title.

In 1862, the Homestead Act was passed, permitting any American citizen, or anyone in the process of becoming a citizen, to file for a quarter section of 160 acres by paying a small registration fee. After he had lived on, cultivated and improved the land for five years, the settler received title to the land.

A tract of land near the center of this map was the first to be claimed. The claimant, Daniel Freeman, traveled for days to reach the Brownville, Nebraska, land office in time for registration.

Compare the settlement with that at Abiquiu, New Mexico. The differences reflect not only the differences in the physical settings of the two but also those in culture. The American farmer of European origin, unlike most farmers of the rest of the world, has never lived in villages. He has built his home on the land he cultivates.

1. The land laws of the United States were aimed at making this a nation of small farms. Explain.
2. Where were most of the "homestead" lands located? Explain.
3. What has been the trend in farm size in the United States in the past several decades? Account for this.
4. Was 160 acres a suitable size for homesteads?
5. Compare land-use in the valley of Cub Creek with that in the valley of the Chama River. Why does this difference exist?
6. Describe the pattern of the roads on the Beatrice quadrangle.

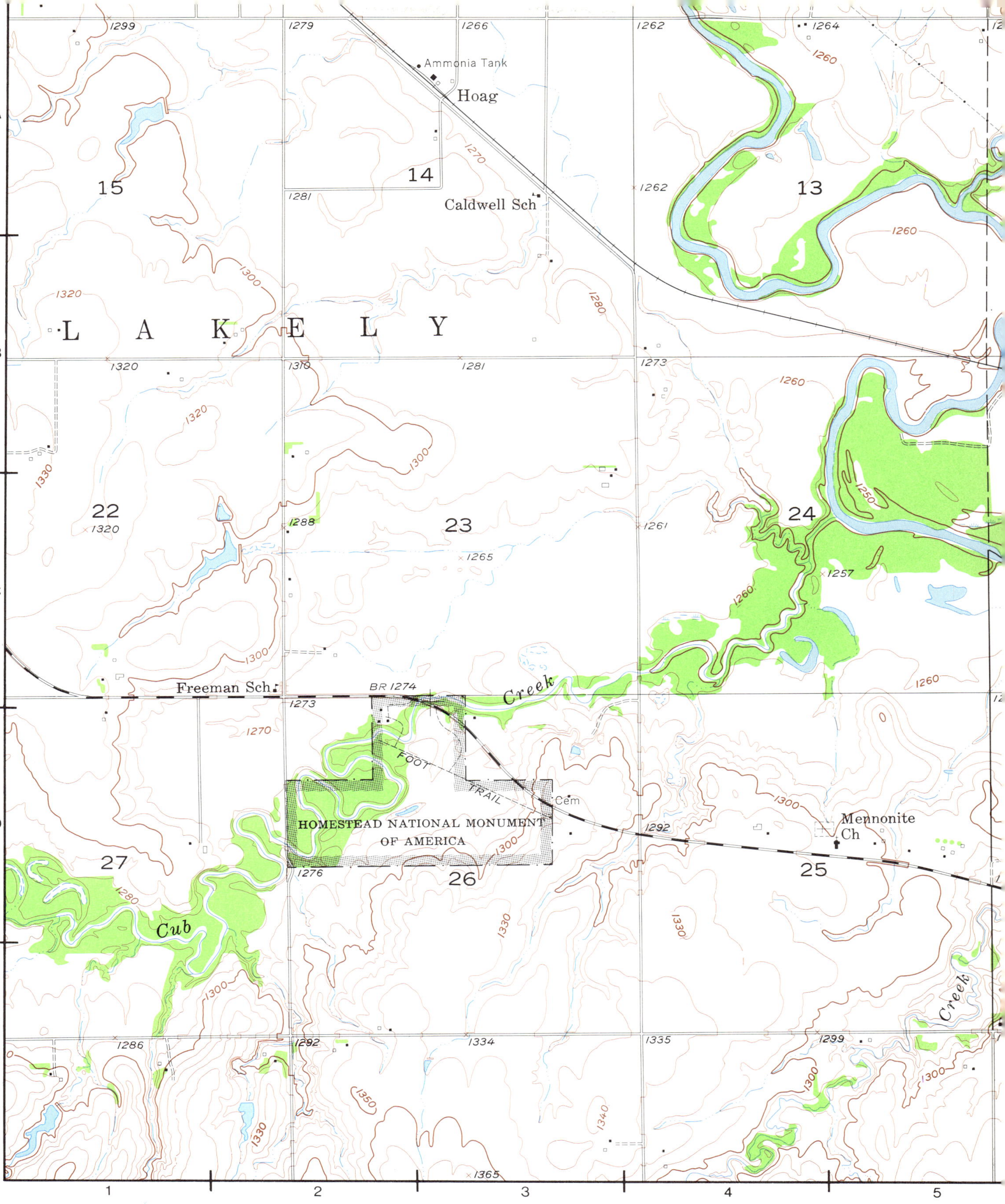

from Beatrice West Quadrangle, Nebraska—Gage Co.

Scale	1:24,000
Contour Interval	10 ft.
Latitude	40° 16′ 30″ N to 40° 19′ 30″ N
Longitude	96° 48′ W to 96° 51′ 30″ W

½ 0 1 MILE

1 .5 0 1 KILOMETER

BLEECKER, ALABAMA

Bleecker is located in the Appalachian Piedmont. Cultivation is confined to the higher land where soils are better drained. Much of the land has been allowed to return to forests.

The early settlers were mainly farmers who cleared and cultivated a tract of land until its soils were depleted and then abandoned the land and cleared another tract. The abandoned land, devoid of its vegetative cover, was soon destroyed by erosion.

The major crop cultivated in the area was cotton, which was well suited to the soils and climate of the area. Little was done, however, to preserve the productivity of the soil, and the yields began to drop. By the beginning of the twentieth century, cotton production had declined. Today the major crop is corn, followed by cotton, peas, beans, peanuts and hay.

The only settlements are Motts and Bleecker; they provide a few services for the sparse local population. Transportation facilities in the north and west of the area are limited to light duty or dirt roads and two railroad lines. The southeast part of the map appears almost uninhabited. Except for a few dirt trails, there are no signs of roads.

1. How is cultivation related to topography?
2. Describe the land use in this area. What crops can you recognize in the cultivated fields?
3. Does the region have good transportation facilities? Explain. How has topography influenced the location of roads?
4. Compare this region with Buckingham, Iowa. State the differences and what they indicate.
5. Was the Township and Range survey completed before or after settlement of this area? Explain.
6. This quadrangle is located in the Red and Yellow Great Soil Group area of the United States. Describe the red and yellow soils. Explain how they were formed. What evidences of soil erosion can be seen in the area?
7. By use of the aerial photograph, describe the vegetation in this area.

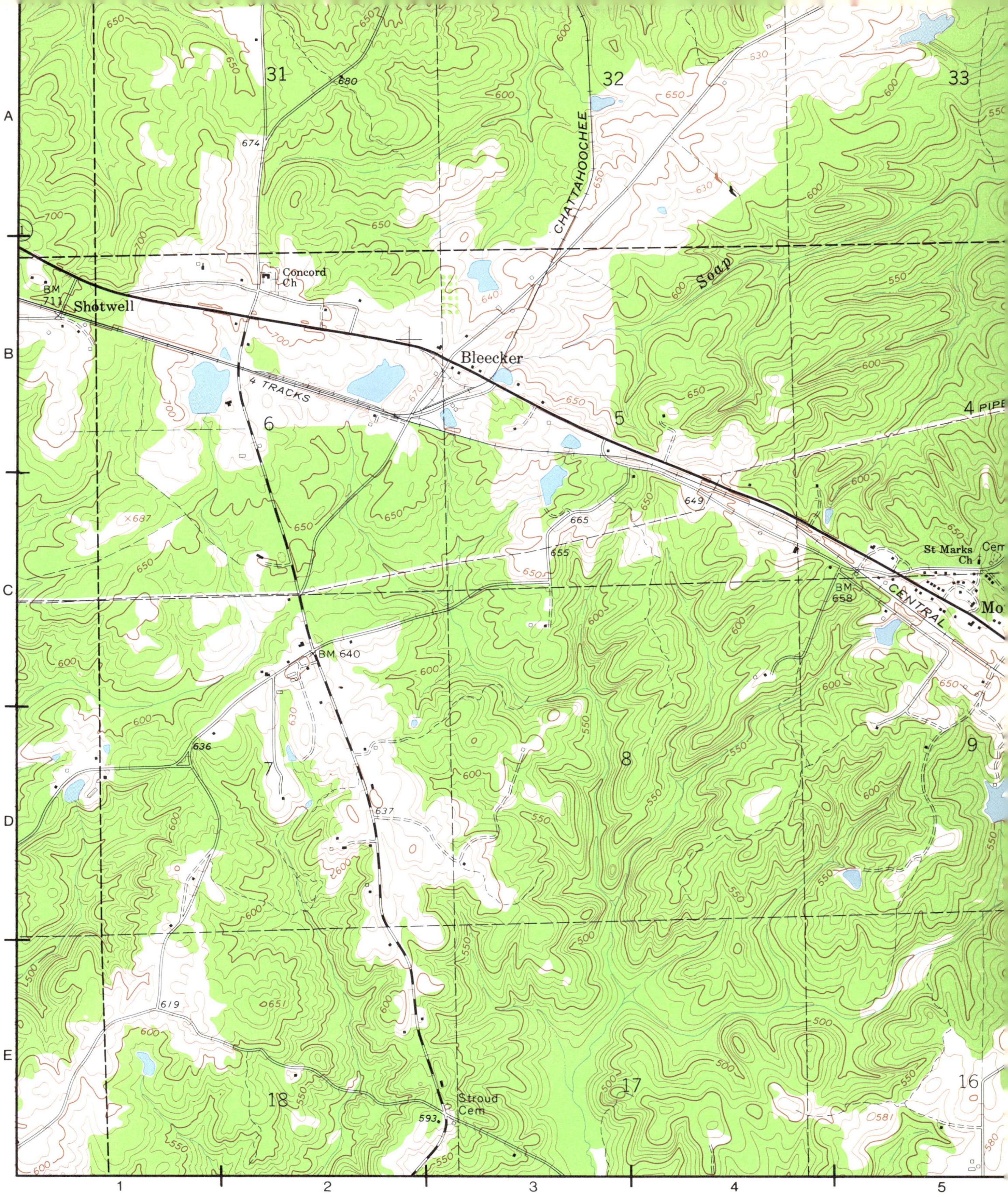

from Bleecker Quadrangle, Alabama—Lee Co.

Scale 1:24,000
Contour Interval 10 ft.
Latitude 32° 33′ N to 32° 36′ N
Longitude 85° 08′ W to 85° 11′ 30″ W

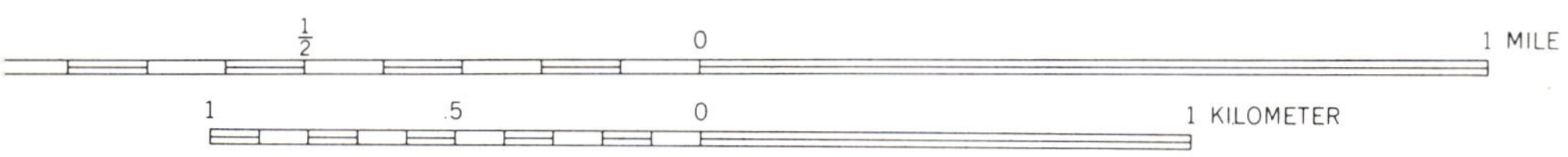

ABIQUIU, NEW MEXICO

The region around Abiquiu (pronounced AB-A-QUE), New Mexico, is the site of one of the early settlements in the United States. The Pueblo Indians, so called because they lived in villages, or pueblos, have occupied these drylands since prehistoric times and cultivated the surrounding land with the help of irrigation. They were already leading a sedentary life when the first Spanish explorers came.

The Spanish conquered this region in 1598 but they did not begin their settlements until around 1744. The first settlement in the region was at Santa Rosa de Abiquiu, about 1¼ miles east of the present village of Abiquiu. Abiquiu was established by the Christian Genizaro Indians who had adopted Spanish customs. The 1200-mile-long Spanish Trail from Santa Fe to California passed through Abiquiu. It took caravans about three months to cover the distance between Abiquiu and California.

The village, like most Spanish settlements, is dominated by the church and monastery. The present-day inhabitants of Abiquiu are mostly farmers who grow corn, cotton, beans and other vegetables in the irrigated valley. The main source of water is the Chama River, a tributary of the Rio Grande. To provide maximum frontage on the river, the fields are divided into long and narrow lots that extend backward from the river. Farms that do not have river frontages receive their water supply by ditches from the river and from wells.

Outside the village, smaller settlements are scattered along the river. Ranching predominates in the area. Water for cattle is obtained from wells.

1. Account for the location of roads in the area of this quadrangle.
2. Compare agriculture around Abiquiu with that around Gila Butte, Arizona. Why is it better developed at Gila Butte? Compare the distribution of cultivated land at the two locations.
3. What is the importance of a location along the Chama River?
4. Describe the distribution of vegetation in this area. From the photograph describe the types of vegetation at different altitudes.
5. What material is used to build houses and other buildings in this area? From where does the material come?
6. How does the map indicate the Spanish influence in this area?
7. In most parts of the country semiarid regions are limited to the activity of raising cattle. Why is cultivation carried on around Abiquiu?

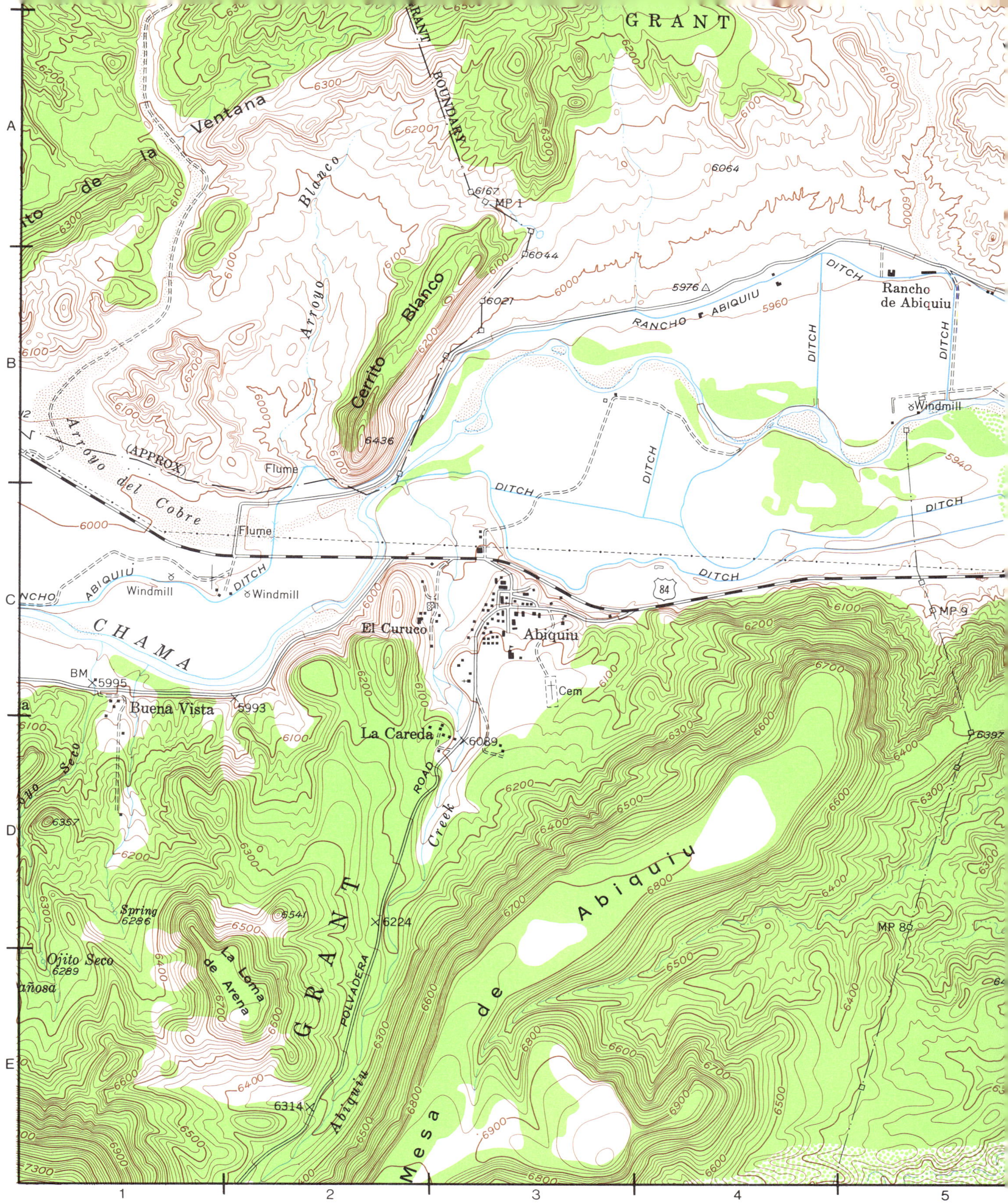

from Abiquiu Quadrangle, New Mexico—Rio Arriba Co.

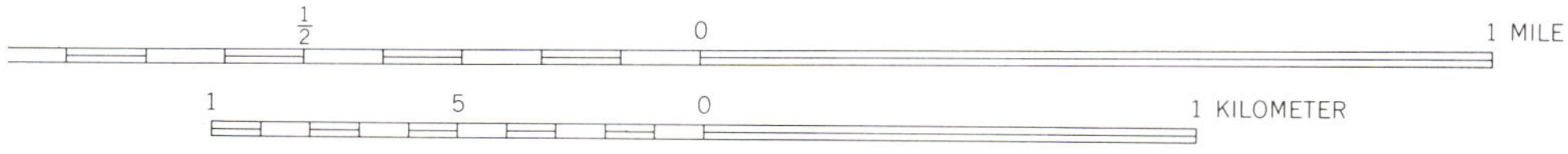

Scale 1:24,000
Contour Interval 20 ft.
Latitude 36° 11′ N to 36° 14′ N
Longitude 106° 17′ 30″ W to 106° 20′ 30″ W

Agricultural Impressions

Although about half of the total acreage in the United States is classified as farmland, only about 17 percent of the land area of the country is cultivated for food and fiber. Man has transformed the countryside into a cultural landscape by his agricultural practices. He has cleared forests, drained swamps and marshes, irrigated drylands, terraced and contoured hills and plowed and fertilized the soils to prepare land for agriculture.

Agricultural impressions are only indirectly apparent on quadrangle maps. Orchards are usually indicated by green dots, but the kind of fruit grown is not revealed. Field boundaries are shown as dashed lines on only some of the more recent quadrangles. Field boundaries in some parts of the country form a regular rectangular pattern, reflecting the Public Land Survey.

Another indirect indication of agricultural practices in an area are ditches. Ditches may be distinguished from streams by their straight courses and angularity of bends. They indicate the presence of an irrigation or drainage system that is often necessary for agriculture. In humid areas, ditches serve as outlets for underground pipes and clay tiles that remove water from poorly drained soils. In dry areas, ditches carry water from wells, streams or reservoirs to the fields. They also carry irrigation water off the fields so that harmful salts will not be precipitated when the water evaporates. Sometimes natural waterways are straightened and deepened.

Another clue to agriculture in an area is the presence of isolated houses and barns that make up the farmstead. Also, windmills and stock ponds scattered over the countryside may be seen on topographic quadrangles. A well-developed system of farm-to-market roads may be present. Small towns may include grain elevators and cattle loaders near a railroad line.

Agriculture is best identified on the aerial photograph. On the aerial photograph the pattern, tone, texture, shape, size, topographic site and association with other objects gives direct information about a cultural feature. The special arrangement of fields, crops and other agricultural objects is apparent. Row crops such as orchards, corn, tobacco or cotton are discernible. The cultivation and harvesting patterns often provide clues to the crop and the agricultural techniques employed.

The tone on black-and-white photographs indicates the stage of crop growth, kind of soil and the degree to which drainage or irrigation is employed. The texture distinguishes coarse crops such as corn, sorghum and pineapples from those that have a fine-textured image such as oats, wheat and sugarcane. Practices such as contour stripping or terracing; structures such as elevators, silos or corn cribs; and farm implements give a clue to the crop being grown. Association with other crops is always an important consideration, as one would not expect to find a field of pineapples adjacent to wheat or an orchard of lemons on a Wisconsin dairy farm.

The maps in this section illustrate several types of agricultural impressions. Others exist, but space has not permitted their inclusion. Aspects of rural settlement, in addition to those discussed in the other sections, are also shown on the following maps.

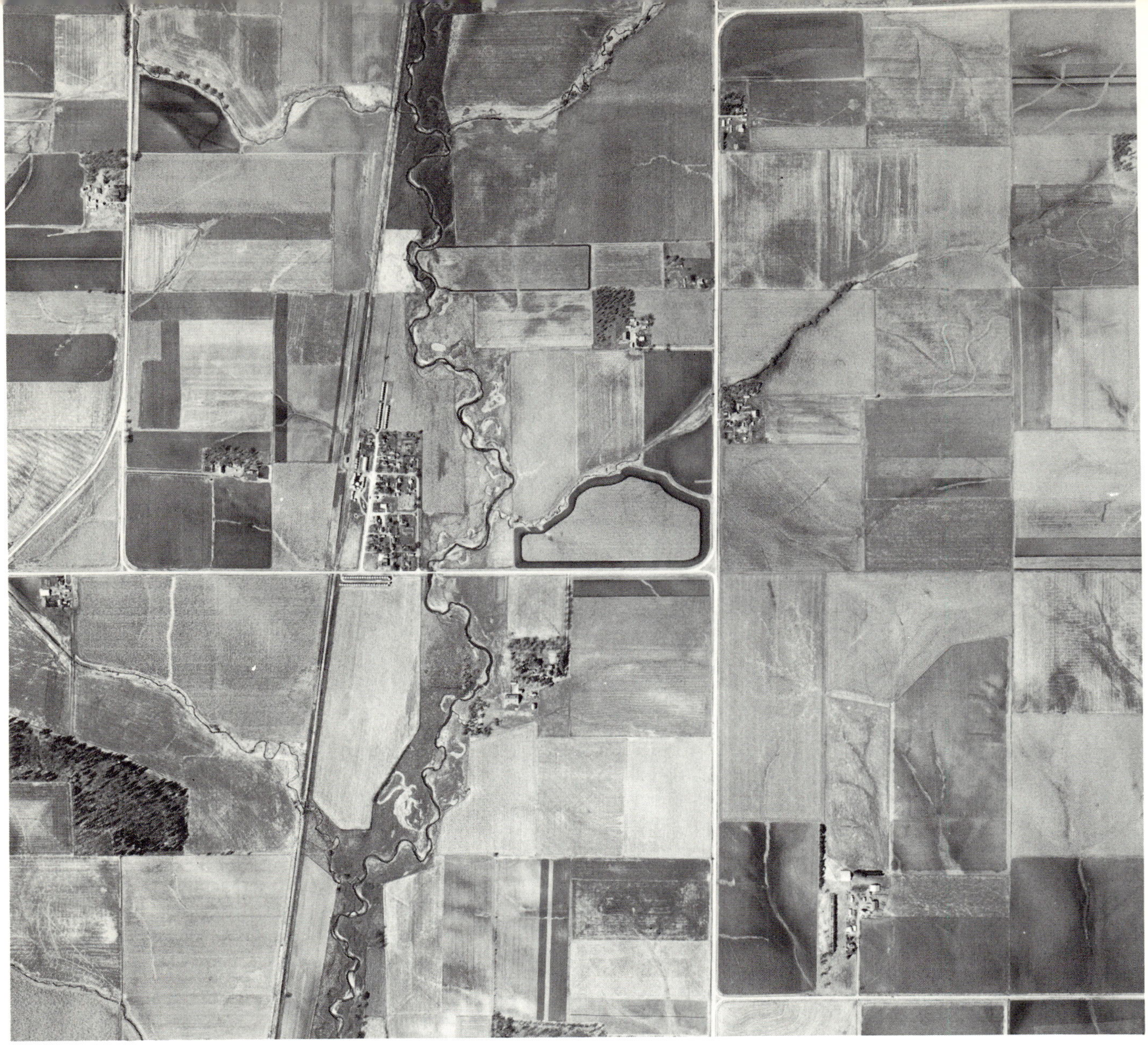

BUCKINGHAM, IOWA

This map represents an area of the American Corn Belt in Central Iowa. The area is representative of areas of Prairie soils, with some Gray-Brown Podzolic soils present. The area lies in the western Young Drift section of the Interior Lowlands. A humid continental climate prevails in the area. The native vegetation in this area was formerly tall prairie grasses, although scattered stands of oak-hickory forests occurred in some upland areas and along stream courses.

Tama County, of which this map represents a part, was organized in 1852. The first settlement was made in 1848. The agriculture was of a subsistence type; however, after the railroad arrived in the area in 1862, the agricultural emphasis shifted to commercial production.

The modern agricultural emphasis is only indirectly illustrated by the map in terms of the absence of forests, regularity and number of farm-to-market roads, and the regularity and wide-spacing of farmsteads, along with indications of field boundaries throughout all sections.

The rural nature of this area is apparent from both the map and the aerial photograph. The aerial photograph shows that almost all of the upland areas are under cultivation. On the aerial photograph corn can be distinguished by tone and texture from the small grains, pasture and soybeans.

The farmsteads are located, for the most part, along the roads. In only a few cases are they situated in the interior of the section and connected to the roads by farm lanes. On the average there are about four farmsteads per section.

1. Identify some of the modern agricultural advancements that are evident on the photograph and map.
2. Describe the farm buildings. What do they indicate about the life of the farmers?
3. Explain the internal drainage conditions of the soils by map and photograph evidences.
4. Account for the lack of forests in this area. Where are the existing forests located? What use is made of them?
5. Contrast agricultural practices around Buckingham, Iowa, with those around Bleecker, Alabama. With the area around Fulton, Indiana.
6. Locate places on the aerial photo where the road pattern differs from that seen on the map. Explain.
7. Compare the field boundaries on the map with those on the aerial photograph. Explain the similarities and differences.
8. What is the only agglomerated settlement in this area? Explain its function.

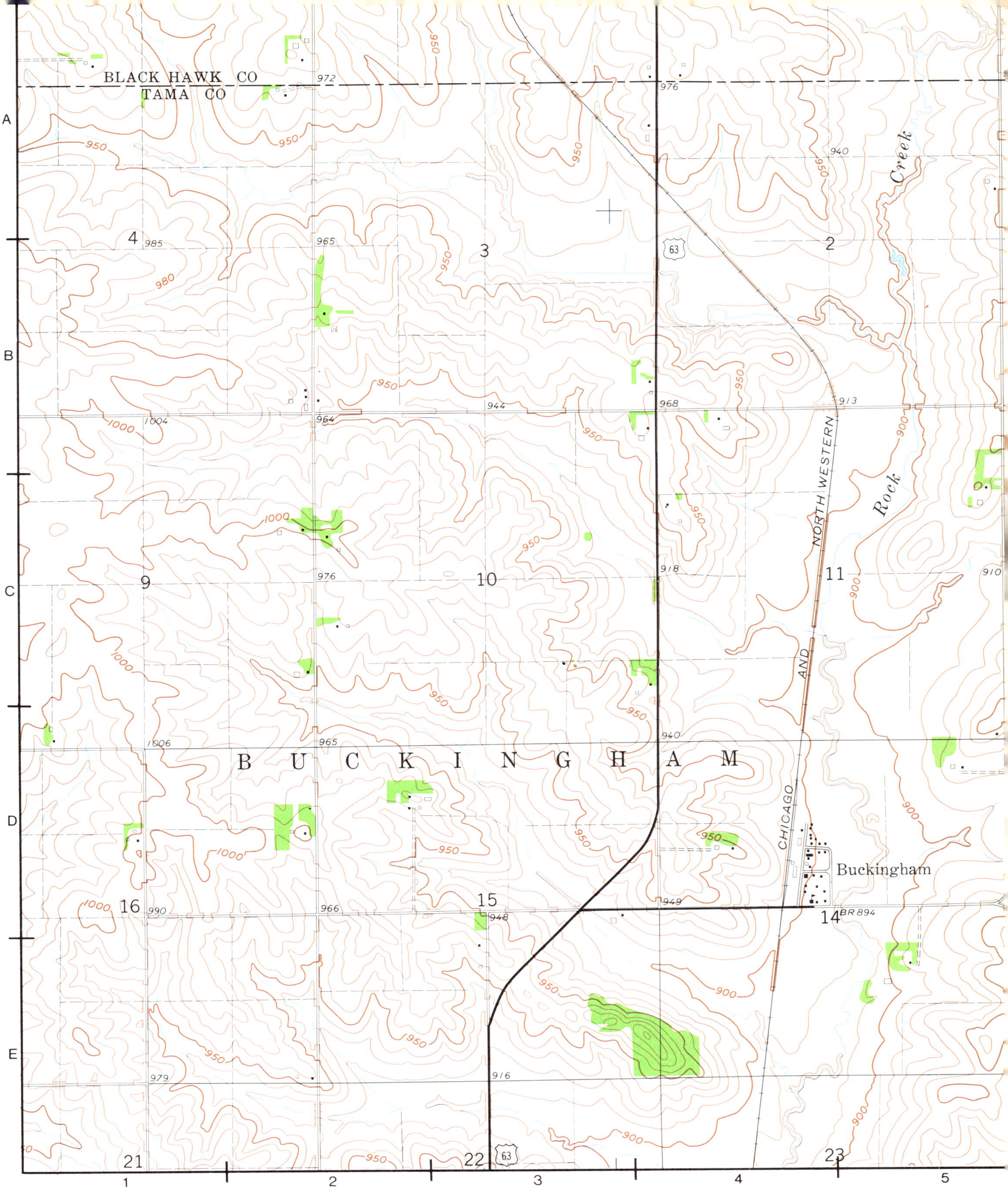

from Buckingham Quadrangle, Iowa

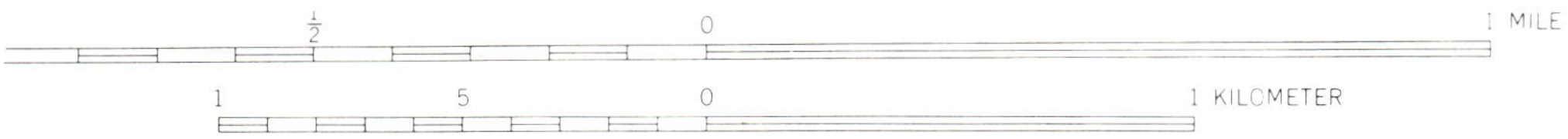

Scale 1:24,000
Contour Interval 10 ft.
Latitude 42° 15′ N
to 42° 18′ N
Longitude 92° 26′ W
to 92° 29′ 30″ W

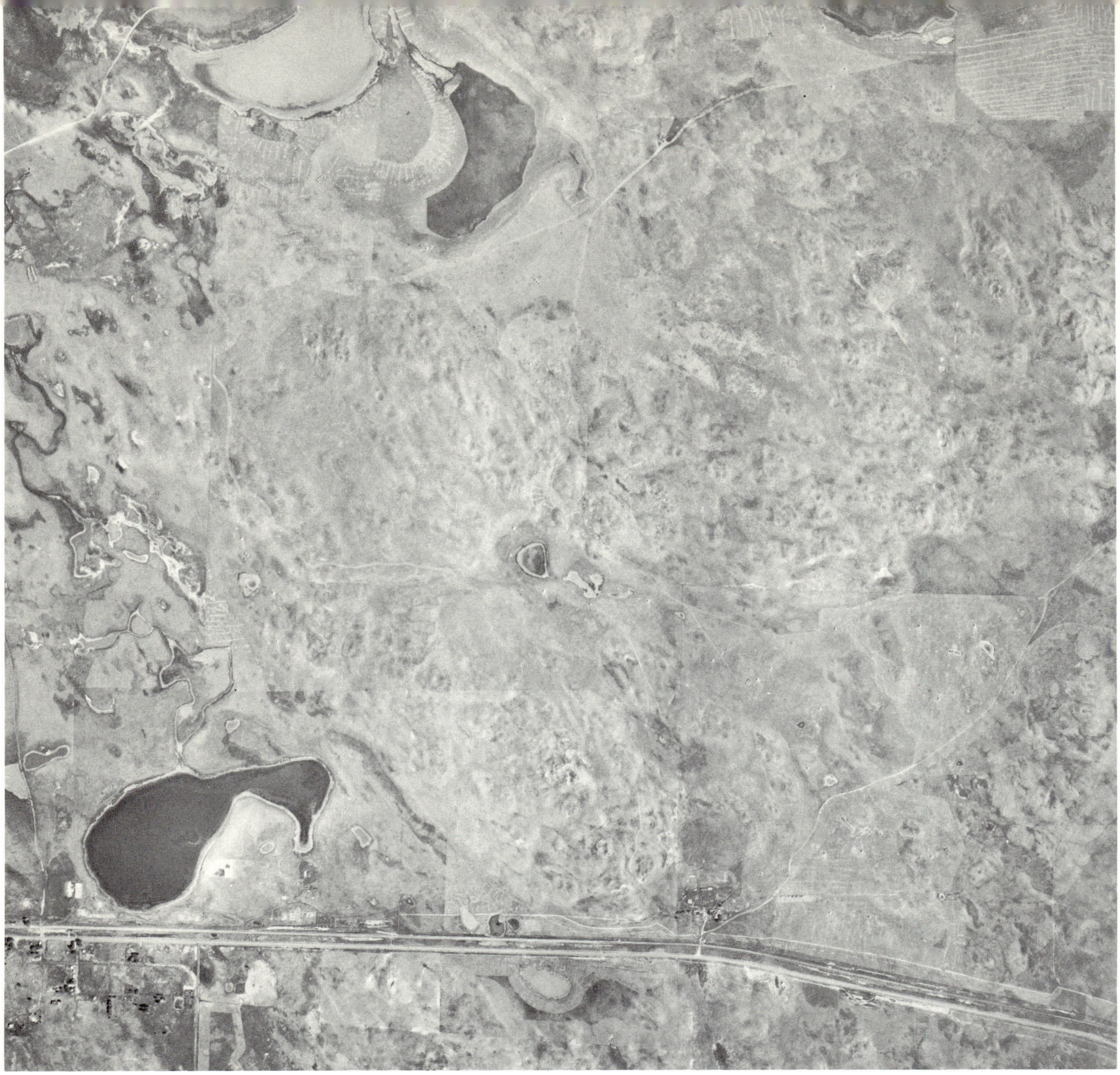

ANTIOCH, NEBRASKA

The Sand Hills of Nebraska make up an 18,000-square-mile tract of stationary sand dunes. The aerial photograph shows that the domical sand dunes have been largely stabilized by a vegetation cover, mostly short bunch grasses.

The low productivity of the sandy soil makes the land best suited to grazing. The type of agriculture carried out in this area is cattle-raising. Much of the range land is unfenced, except along the highway and railroad. The windmills utilize wind energy for pumping ground water and insure sweet water for the cattle herds. Wild hay is cut from the depressions and hill slopes for winter feeding.

For the most part the landscape in the Sand Hills is desolate. With the exception of Nebraska State Highway 2, all the roads are light-duty dirt roads or trails. Many of them are barely distinguishable on the photograph.

The sections of the Public Land Survey are shown on the map. Because meridians converge toward the poles, survey lines cannot be parallel throughout and occasional corrections are needed. Such a correction can be seen on this map north of Antioch.

The single track of the Burlington Railroad passes through the hamlet of Antioch. A cattle-loading siding may be seen on the north side of the railroad tracks at Antioch.

1. Why are the dunes very dry when the depressions are swampy? What is the nature of the water in the depressions and lakes between the sand dunes? Explain.
2. Are the farmsteads located on top of the dunes or in the depressions? Explain.
3. What is the use of the trees that cluster around the structures?
4. Is the region well served with transportation facilities?
5. The Indian Village of Abiquiu, New Mexico, has a dry climate like Antioch, Nebraska. Yet the Abiquiu farmer raises beans and vegetables while the Antioch farmer raises cattle. Give a reason for the difference.
6. Explain the name School Section Lakes in Sections 16 and 21; T25N; R45W.

from Antioch Quadrangle, Nebraska

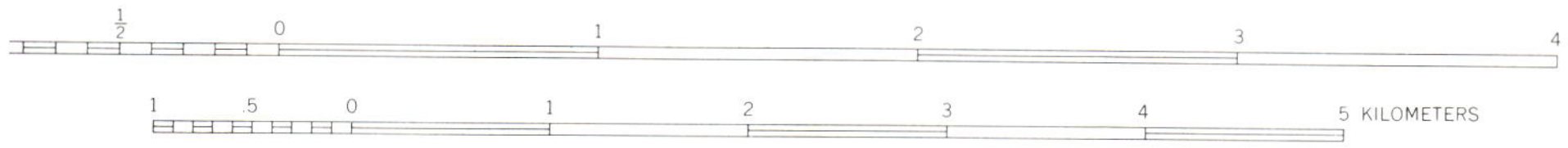

Scale 1:62,500
Contour Interval 20 ft.
Latitude 42° 02′ N to 42° 10′ N
Longitude 102° 31′ W to 102° 40′ W

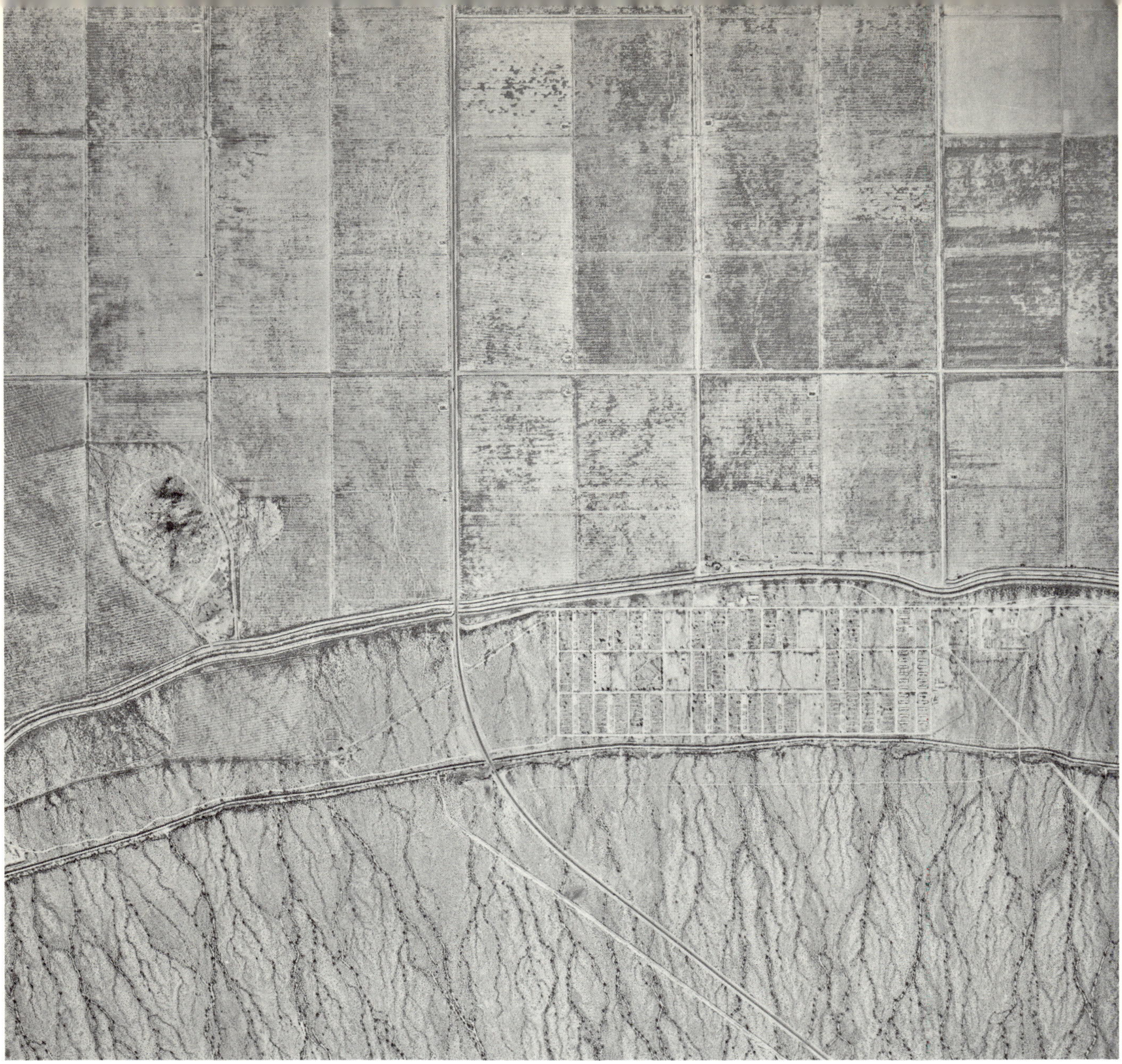

GILA BUTTE, ARIZONA

The area represented by this map is a part of the Sonoran Desert section of the Basin and Range physiographic province. The area is representative of the Red Desert Great Soil Group region, characterized by a hot desert climate and sparse desert vegetation. The aerial photograph indicates that the area remains in its original desert condition. Trees are confined to the areas along stream courses while most of the upland areas are blanketed by shrubs.

Although the area was explored by the Spanish in the sixteenth century, settlement did not begin until around 1865. Active settlement and agricultural development did not take place until 1886 when a canal company was formed.

Moisture is the factor limiting plant growth in this area and irrigation water is an absolute necessity for agriculture. Even the early Indian settlers in this area developed crude irrigation works in order to cultivate corn, beans and squash. Cotton occupies the largest acreage under cultivation in this area, followed by alfalfa, wheat, barley, and vegetables, in that order. For the county as a whole, the farm sizes are large, averaging close to one square mile (or 640 acres) in extent. On the other hand, only between 10 to 12 percent of the farm area is improved. Rural settlements in many areas are centered around a church or school.

1. What evidence do you see on the map that indicates the region is very dry? On the aerial photograph?
2. Name some features that indicate irrigation on both the map and aerial photograph.
3. Why do the roads form an almost perfect rectangular grid in the valley but not on the higher land?
4. Both Gila Butte, Arizona, and Keeler, California, are in the desert but land use differs. Explain.
5. What use is made of alfalfa? How did the completion of Coolidge Dam aid agriculture in this area?

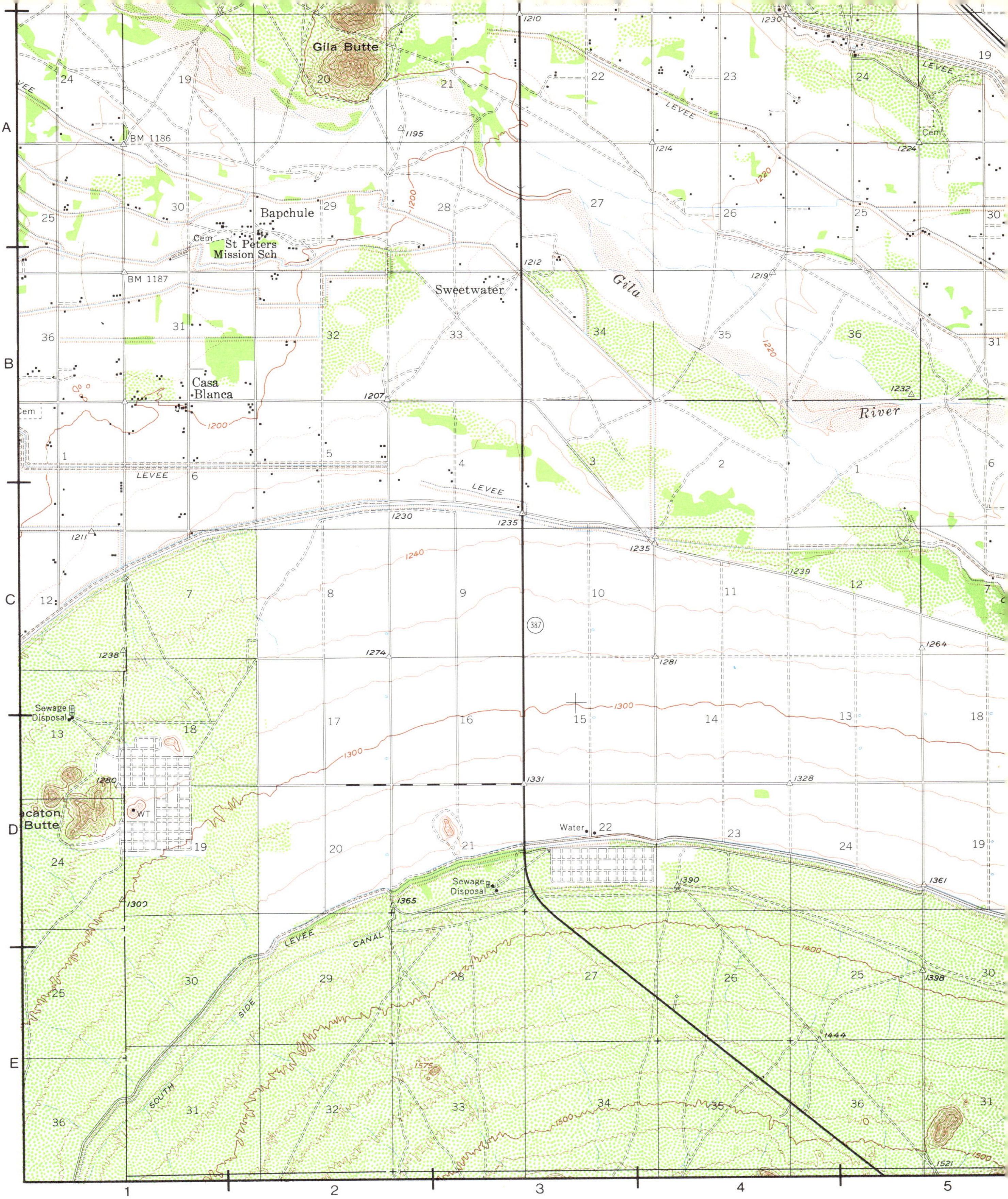

from Gila Butte Quadrangle, Arizona

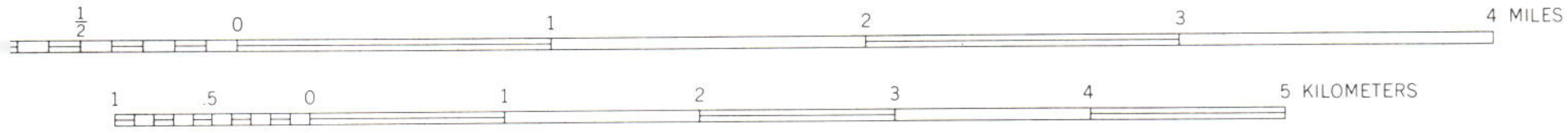

Scale 1:62,500
Contour Interval 20 ft.
Latitude 33° 02′ N
to 33° 10′ N
Longitude 111° 46′ 30″ W
to 111° 54′ 30″ W

HILO, HAWAII

The east slopes of Mauna Loa on the island of Hawaii are planted in sugarcane. When Captain Cook arrived in Hawaii in 1788 he found sugarcane already growing there. Today, it is the most important crop of the state.

The uniformly hot, humid climate and the fertile volcanic soils make the area ideally suited to sugarcane, a tropical to subtropical plant mainly used for the manufacture of sugar. Its stalks grow 10 to 15 feet in height and about 2 inches in diameter. In parts of Hawaii the uniformly heavy rainfall throughout the year permits cane cultivation without irrigation. The area represented on this map receives between 150 and 200 inches of rainfall annually.

At harvest the cane fields are usually set afire to burn the leaves and the older cane. In the wet soil areas hand-cutting is the major method of harvesting, aided by mechanical loaders. Since sugarcane is perishable, it must be processed within a few days of harvest. Therefore, after harvest it is transported to the processing plant immediately. No railroads are visible on the map and photograph in the cane area. Trains are seldom used to transport cane to Hawaiian mills. Cane is sometimes flumed to mills, thus minimizing soil damage by eliminating heavy vehicles from the wet soil areas of the cane fields, but the numerous roads in this area suggest that the cane is mainly transported by trucks.

The only major settlement in the area is Keaau. It provides social, cultural and commercial services for the cane growers and the mill workers.

1. Locate the sugar mill. What activities are carried out in different parts of the mill?
2. What is the difference in the products of this sugar mill and the one in Arecibo, Puerto Rico? What evidences of these differences can you see on the map and photograph?
3. The photograph shows the presence of the fine-textured crop, sugarcane, while the map indicates the presence of an orchard. Give a reason for the discrepancy.
4. Describe the forest vegetation in this area. Compare it to the area around Arecibo, Puerto Rico. Compare the rainfall in this area with that of the Arecibo area in Puerto Rico.
5. In the areas indicated as shrub on the map, guava is a characteristic plant. What is guava?
6. From what source does Keaau obtain its water supply?
7. What is the source of fuel in the sugar mill?

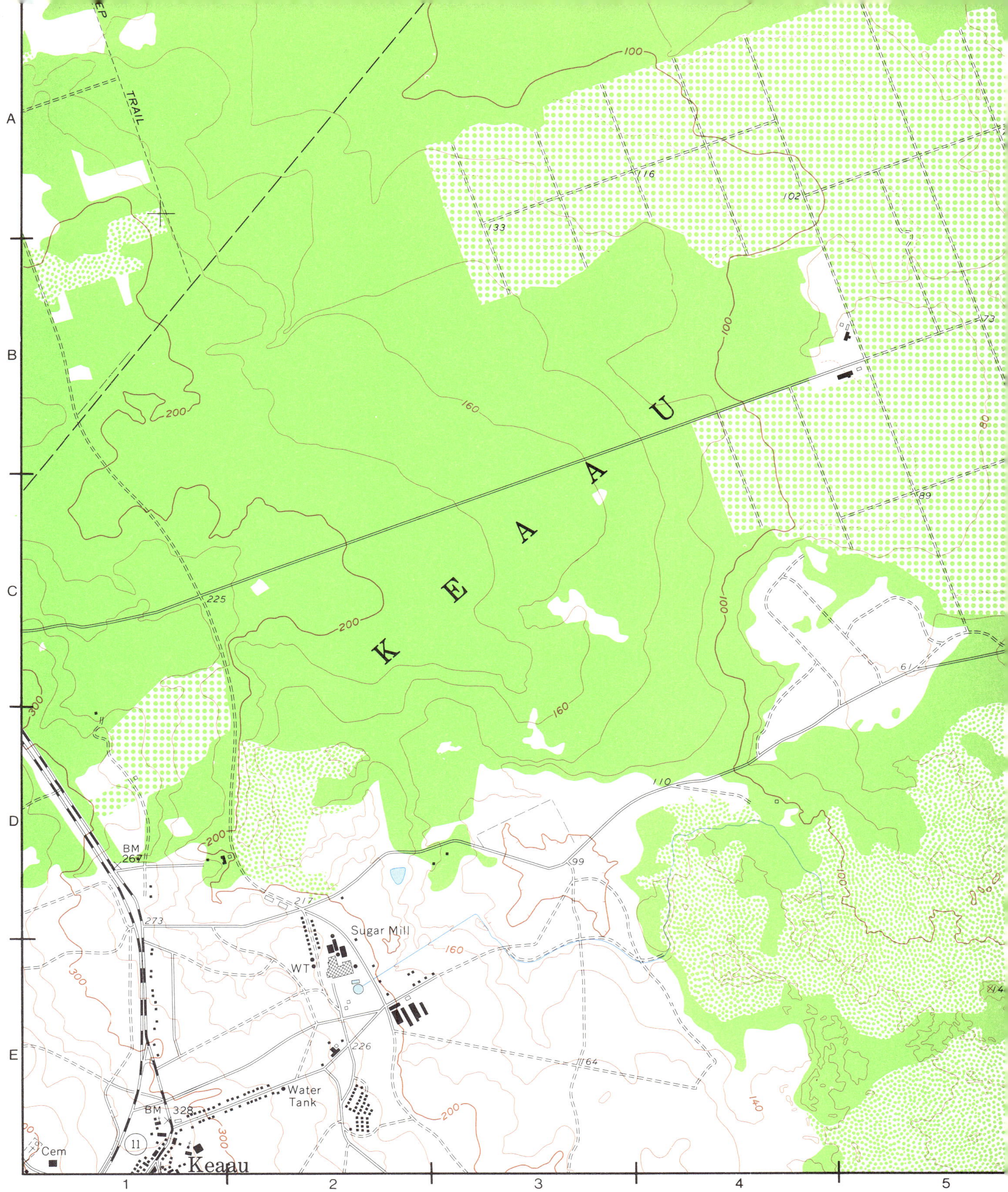

from Hilo Quadrangle, Hawaii—Island and County of Hawaii

Scale 1:24,000
Contour Interval 20 ft.
Latitude 19° 37′ 30″ N to 19° 40′ 30″ N
Longitude 155° W to 155° 03′ W

1/2 0 1 MILE

1 .5 0 1 KILOMETER

ARECIBO, PUERTO RICO

This map shows an area of tropical agriculture on the northwestern coast of Puerto Rico. The lowlands have been cleared of forests and artificially drained to make room for highly valuable cash crops, such as sugarcane and pineapples. Agriculture is possible only with extensive water control measures, which insure proper irrigation and drainage.

You can see from the map and photograph that most of the coastal region is poorly drained. Because the area is subject to overflow, the "grand-bank" system of cane cultivation is used. The land is shaped into alternate ditches and ridges and the sugarcane is planted in rows along the ridges. During wet or overflow periods the ditches provide drainage, and during drought they provide irrigation.

Most of the cane is a volunteer, or ratoon, crop. At harvest, only the stems above the ground are cut. The runners underground remain to generate another crop. Ratoon crops may regenerate for as long as eight years. Thus, annual soil preparation and planting are eliminated.

The harvesting season in Puerto Rico begins in January and lasts until June. The fields are burned to remove the leaves and the cane is cut by hand with a machete. The cane is then transported to the centrales, where it is processed.

At the mill, the cane is crushed for juice, which is evaporated to crystallized crude sugar. The mill in the photograph distills the sugar and molasses for rum.

The gently rolling plain, south of the cane fields, is cultivated for pineapples. They are harvested about 12 to 22 months after planting. Pineapples are planted in rows and require considerable hand labor during growth and harvest.

1. Where in the mapped area are lands artificially drained?
2. How is the cane transported from the fields to the mills? Substantiate your answer from features on the map and photograph.
3. How can you distinguish between fields of sugarcane and pineapples on the aerial photograph?
4. How many small villages can you see in this area? What is their function?
5. Compare the agricultural practices at Arecibo with those on Hilo, Hawaii.
6. Explain the distribution of the forests in the mapped area. Compare the vegetation on the aerial photograph with the areas of vegetation on the map. Explain.

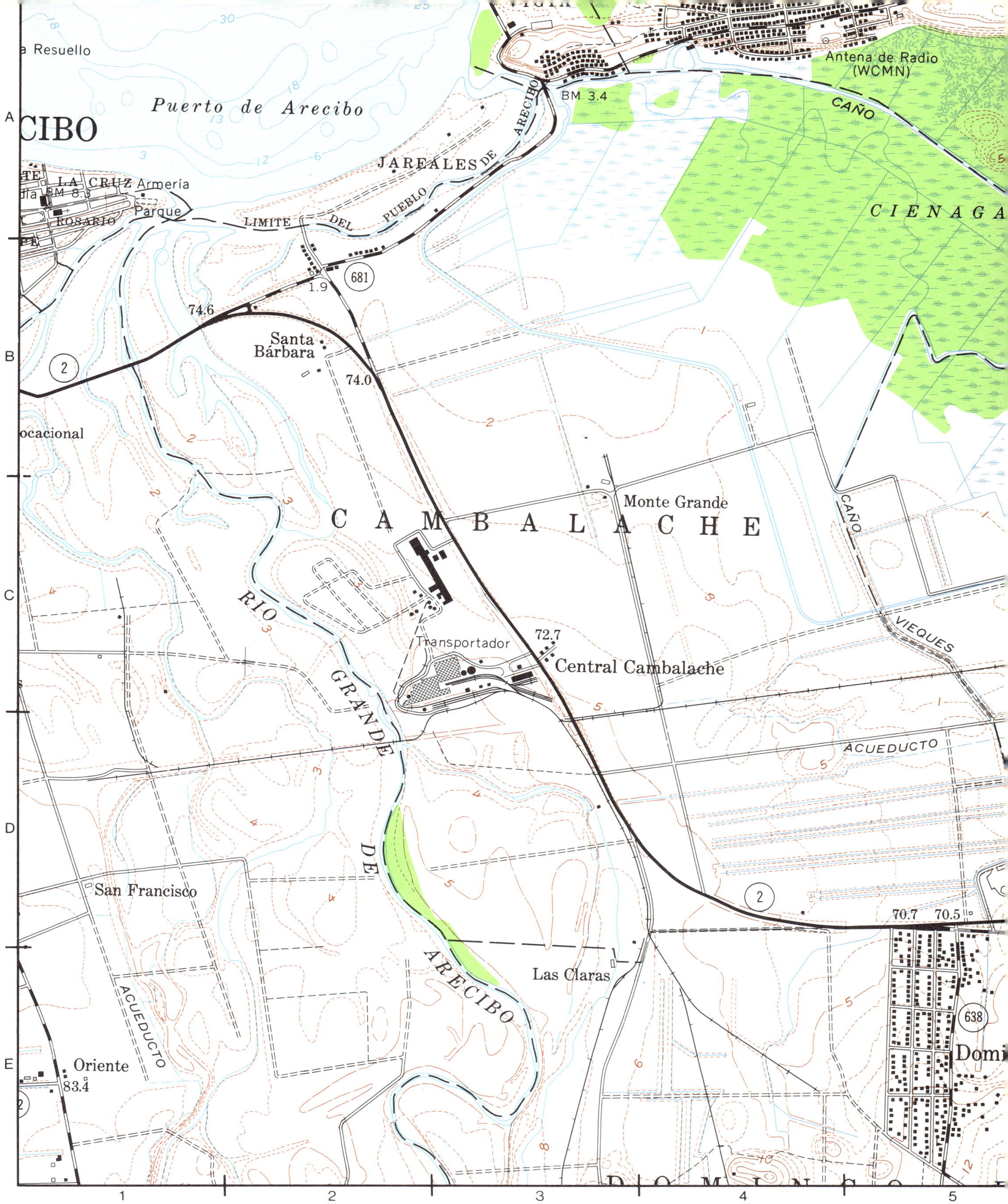

from Arecibo Quadrangle, Puerto Rico—Municipio de Arecibo

Scale 1:20,000
Contour Interval 10 m.

Latitude 18° 26′ 30″ N to 18° 29′ N
Longitude 66° 41′ W to 66° 43′ W

$\frac{1}{2}$ 0 1 MILE

1 .5 0 1 KILOMETER

Industrial Impressions

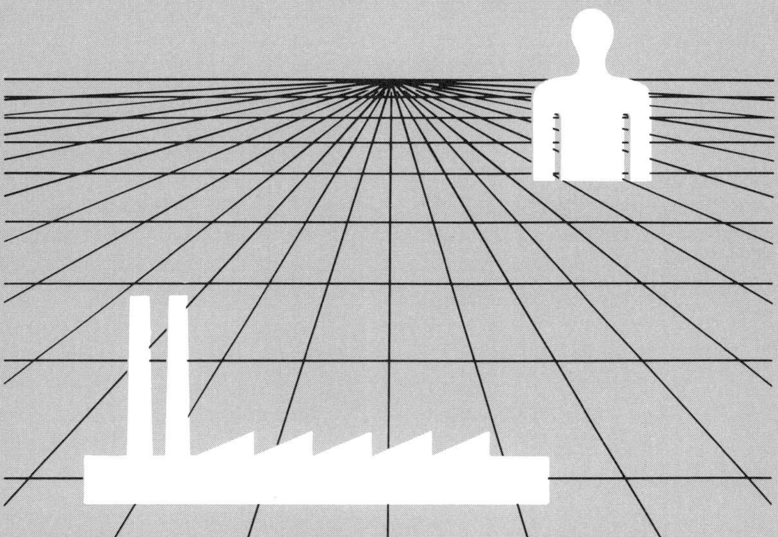

While agriculture is disseminated over large areas of the countryside, industry tends to be concentrated where raw materials, capital, labor and transportation are available. Most industries are closely associated with large urban areas and employ the bulk of their inhabitants. Nearly 20 million people of the United States are employed in manufacturing industries and nearly 630,000 people in mining industries.

Industry not only occupies the majority of the people and makes up the bulk of the gross national product, but its impressions mark a major way by which man has modified the face of the earth in local areas. Mines, oil fields and industrial concentrations drastically modify the face of the land. Impressions of extractive industries are evident on five of the following maps and those of manufacturing industries on three. Large manufacturing industries, since they are concentrated in urban areas, can also be observed on maps of Urban Impressions and on some maps of Transportation Impressions. Industries related to agriculture may be observed in the section on Agricultural Impressions.

Cultural features related to industry, such as railroad yards, storage tanks, docks, power stations and warehouses, suggest the presence of industrial activities. Most of these features are shown on maps by pictographs, which resemble the objects they illustrate. Industrial buildings and warehouses appear as large, black, crosshatched or shaded rectangles. All the symbols are explained in the key to the maps.

Mining areas appear as distinctive features on topographic maps. The scars of strip-mining and open-pit mining are obvious and leave little doubt that ores or fuels are being removed from the earth. Underground mining, however, is indicated by a symbol for the shaft or tunnel opening. Such features as powerhouses, transmission lines, processing structures, transportation networks and tailings are associated with large mining operations.

The presence of industry may easily be identified on the aerial photograph. Industrial buildings are large, more widely spaced, and usually have smoke stacks, monitor roofs and ventilators. Details of industrial operations are clear to the skilled photograph reader who is able to associate industrial processes with the structures in which they take place. The knowledge of associated equipment, stock piles and other facilities may lend further insight into the processes. Industries are usually closely associated with transportation facilities, such as railroads or canals, and storage facilities, such as stock piles, silos, warehouses and tanks. Older industries are usually located in the inner city, while newer industries are found farther toward its periphery.

Hydroelectric plants are found near dams and are associated with transformer yards, transmission lines and towers, which can be identified on both topographic maps and aerial photographs.

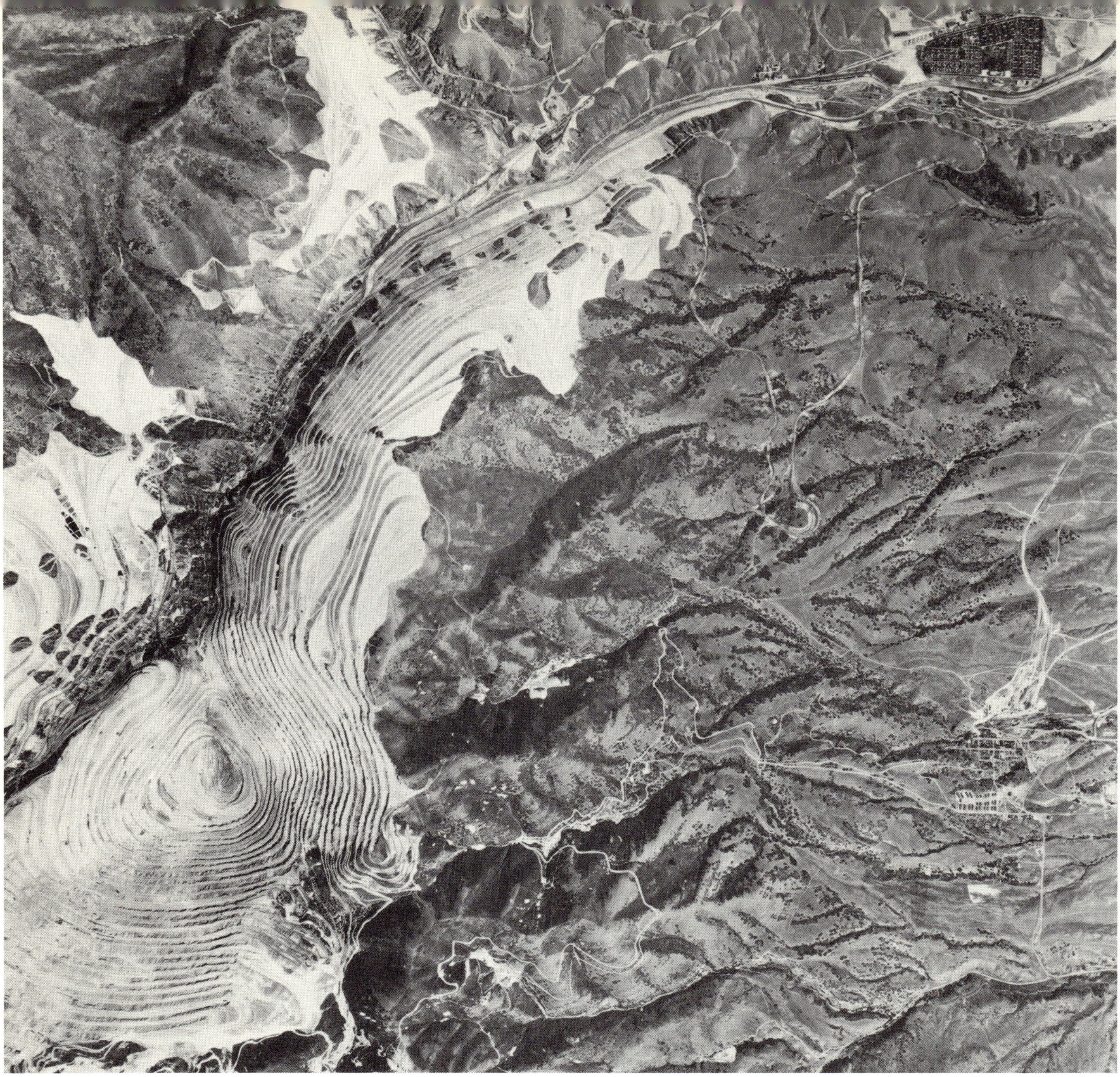

BINGHAM CANYON, UTAH

The mine at Bingham, Utah, is a good example of how man's activities have altered the surface of the earth. Within three-quarters of a century, man has accomplished what nature would have taken hundreds of thousands of years to do. He has removed an entire mountain and created a deep pit in its place. This pit is now the largest open-pit mine in the world, and one of the most important sources of copper in the United States.

The mining operations have converted a mountain of copper porphyry into an amphitheaterlike depression over 1,500 feet deep and more than 2 miles in diameter. The mined ore is loaded into ore cars and carried to the base of the pit, from which trains transport it to processing plants. All operations are electrified.

The ore occurs mostly as pyrite disseminated in monzonite. Although it is low-grade, averaging about 1 percent metallic copper, the mining operation is profitable because modern efficient methods permit cheap handling of enormous quantities of ore. More than 2 billion tons of ore have been removed from this mine since operations began. In addition to copper, the mine produces gold, molybdenum and silver.

1. Why are the sides of the pit terraced?
2. What is the use of the railroad tracks on the terraces?
3. Describe and explain the pattern of Bingham. What restricts the expansion of Bingham and other communities in this area?
4. What has happened to the waste material that was removed from the pit?
5. Would electricity be easily available in the area?
6. What features associated with mining cannot be observed on the photograph, but are labeled on the map? What ore processing features can be seen in this area?
7. Why can ores of only 1 percent metallic copper be mined profitably? (Consider the uses to which copper is put.)

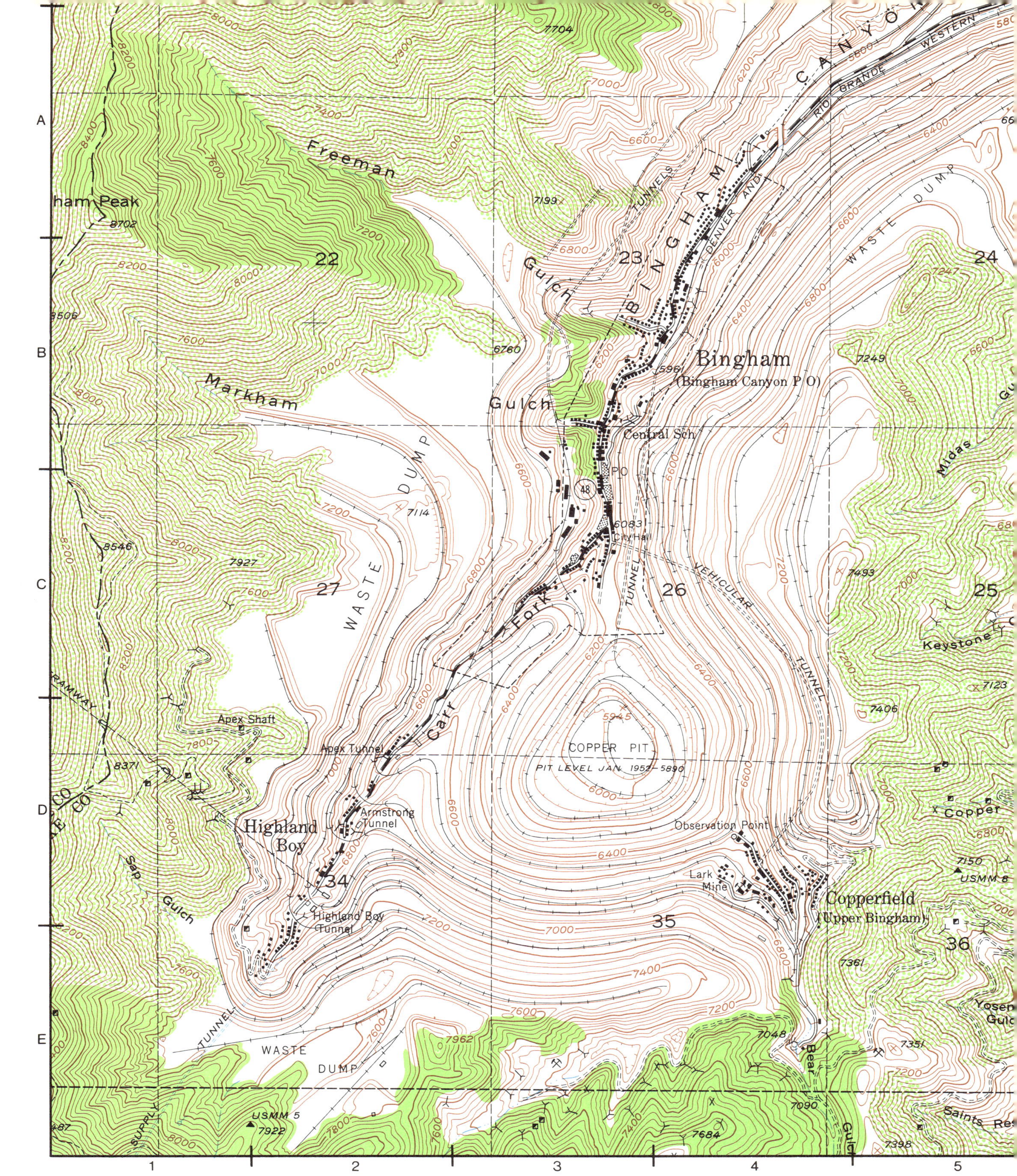

from Bingham Canyon Quadrangle, Utah

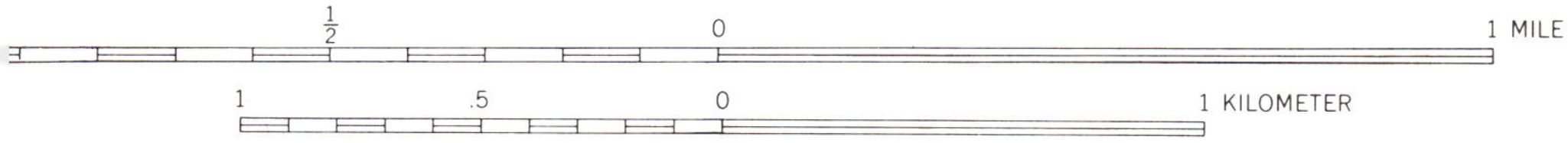

Scale 1:24,000
Contour Interval 40 ft.
Latitude 40° 30′ 30″ N to 40° 33′ 30″ N
Longitude 112° 07′ 30″ W to 112° 11′ W

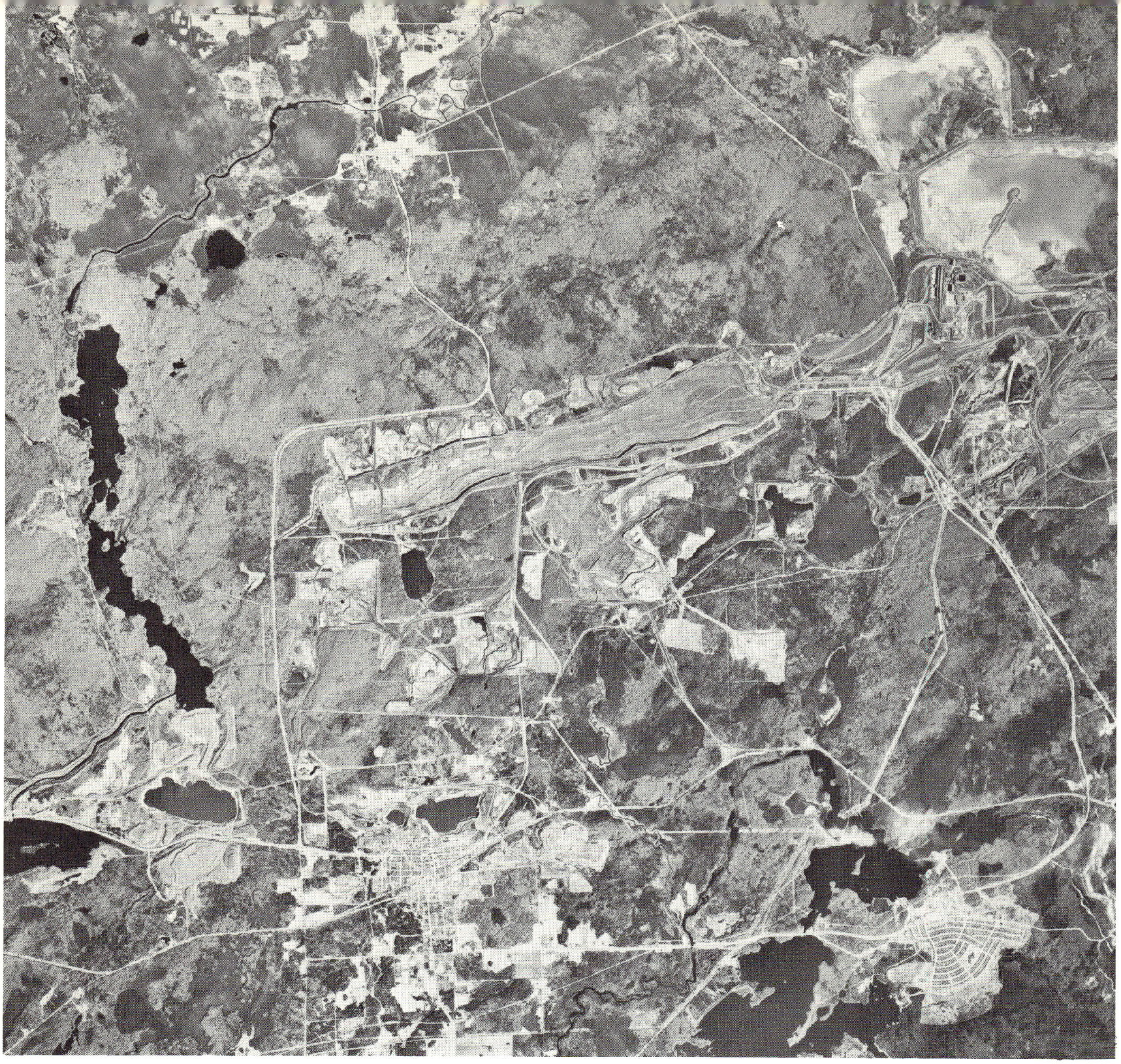

AURORA, MINNESOTA

The mine near Aurora, Minnesota, is another example of man and his machine as the greatest erosive force on earth today. The large scale open-pit mining operations that have become possible with modern technology are responsible for the removal of vast quantities of earth materials. These operations, since they make the exploitation of low-grade ores economically possible, have been man's answer to the dwindling natural resources of the earth.

Taconite is the parent rock from which high-grade hematite and magnetite ores were derived by natural processes of weathering and ground water concentration. Taconite is abundant in the Lake Superior area, but it contains only about 25 to 35 percent metallic iron. In addition, the iron minerals are firmly embedded in silica and other minerals, making the ore difficult to mine.

The difficulties in extraction have been overcome by the use of jet-flame mining processes, and the shipping costs have been reduced by concentrating the ores at the mining site. In 1964, Minnesota strengthened the industry by giving it tax relief.

The taconite ores are transported to the processing plant where they are crushed into three-inch fragments and eventually pulverized. The iron-bearing portions are separated from the gangue of silica and clay and formed into pellets for shipment.

1. Where is the processing plant located? What features indicate the types of processing taking place here?
2. How is the ore transported from the mine to the plant?
3. What other cultural features on the map are associated with mining?
4. What happens to the ore after it leaves the mine? Refer to Superior, Wisconsin, and Gary, Indiana.
5. Locate new settlements which have been built in this area. (Refer to the photograph.) Estimate the population of the settlement east of Whitewater Lake.
6. Explain why many swamps occur in this area.
7. Even the low-grade taconite iron ores contain more metal than the copper ores at Bingham Canyon, Utah. Why would it not be profitable to mine 1 percent iron ore? (Consider the uses to which iron ore is put.)

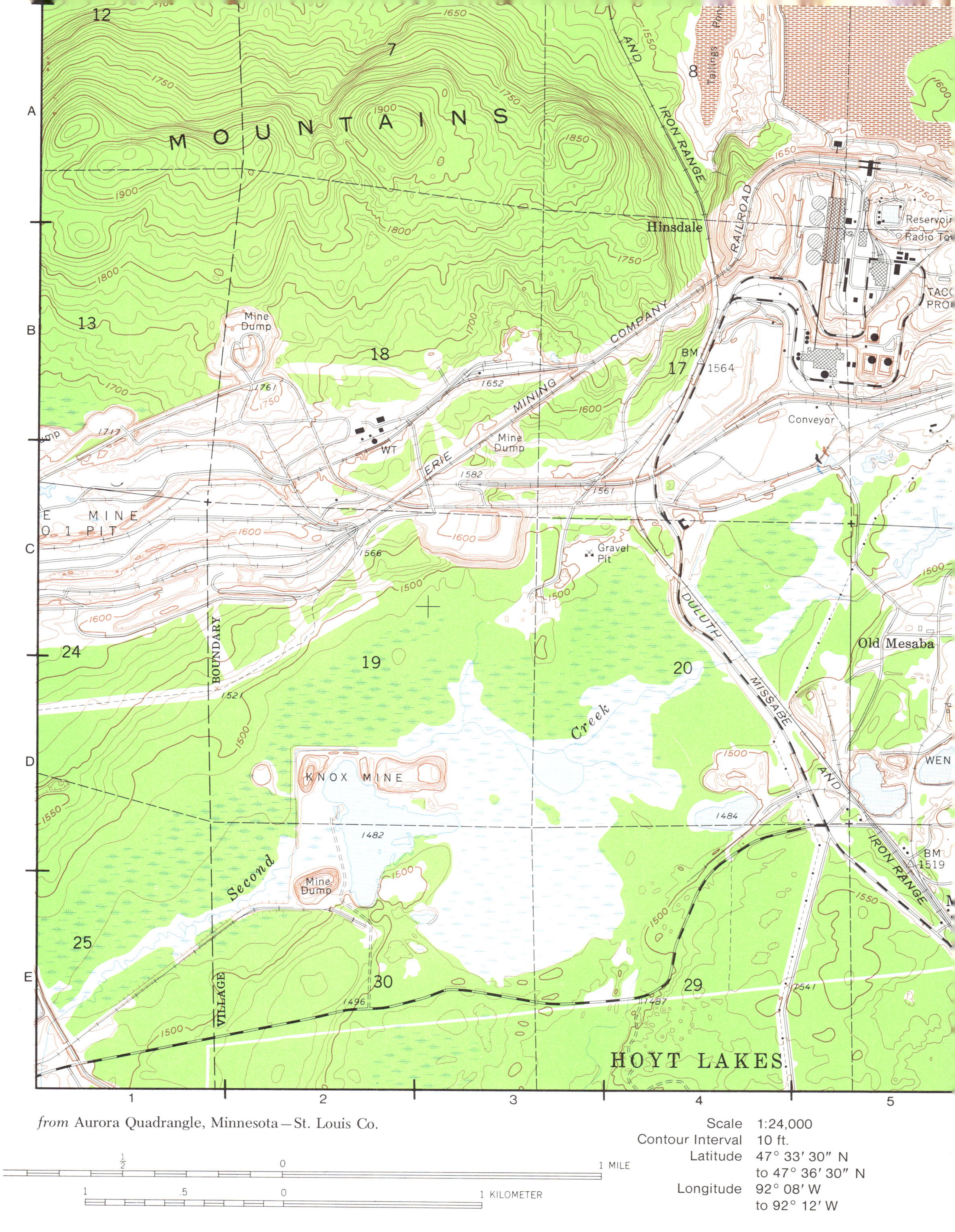

from Aurora Quadrangle, Minnesota—St. Louis Co.

Scale 1:24,000
Contour Interval 10 ft.
Latitude 47° 33′ 30″ N to 47° 36′ 30″ N
Longitude 92° 08′ W to 92° 12′ W

HIBBING, MINNESOTA

Hibbing is located in the heart of the Mesabi Iron Range, which is one of the richest iron-bearing regions of the world. The rich hematite iron ores lie near the surface beneath a thin layer of glacial drift, which makes open-pit mining feasible. The largest open-pit iron mine in the world is located northwest of Hibbing and occupies nearly 13,000 acres. After World War I, mining operations proceeded so rapidly that Hibbing had to be moved one mile farther south. The former site of Hibbing is now occupied by a pit more than 400 feet deep.

The hematite ores, which originally contained over 60 percent iron, were soon depleted, and operations had to turn to poorer but more abundant ores. These ores can be mined profitably in modern times because of modern machinery that is able to remove large quantities of material at comparatively little cost. After the ore at Hibbing is mined, it is taken to crushers and beneficiators where it is concentrated before shipping. Although most of the mining is of the open-pit type, a few shaft mines still exist.

1. How is the ore transported from the mine to the processing plant?
2. What is a mine dump? A tailing pond? Identify these features on the photograph before drawing your conclusion.
3. Why do some roads on the map appear to end abruptly at no particular point?
4. Compare the mined areas on this photograph to those on the map of Coal City, Illinois. Do you see any signs of attempts to restore the land in this area?
5. Suggest reasons why the old cemetery was not molested when the city of Hibbing was moved.
6. Explain the erratic and poor orientation of the Public Land Survey lines in this area. How have these lines affected cultural patterns?
7. Locate the Laurentian Divide on the map. The Three Way Watershed Marker can be located on the aerial photograph 1200 feet west of the light-duty road west of Lavinia. Explain these features.

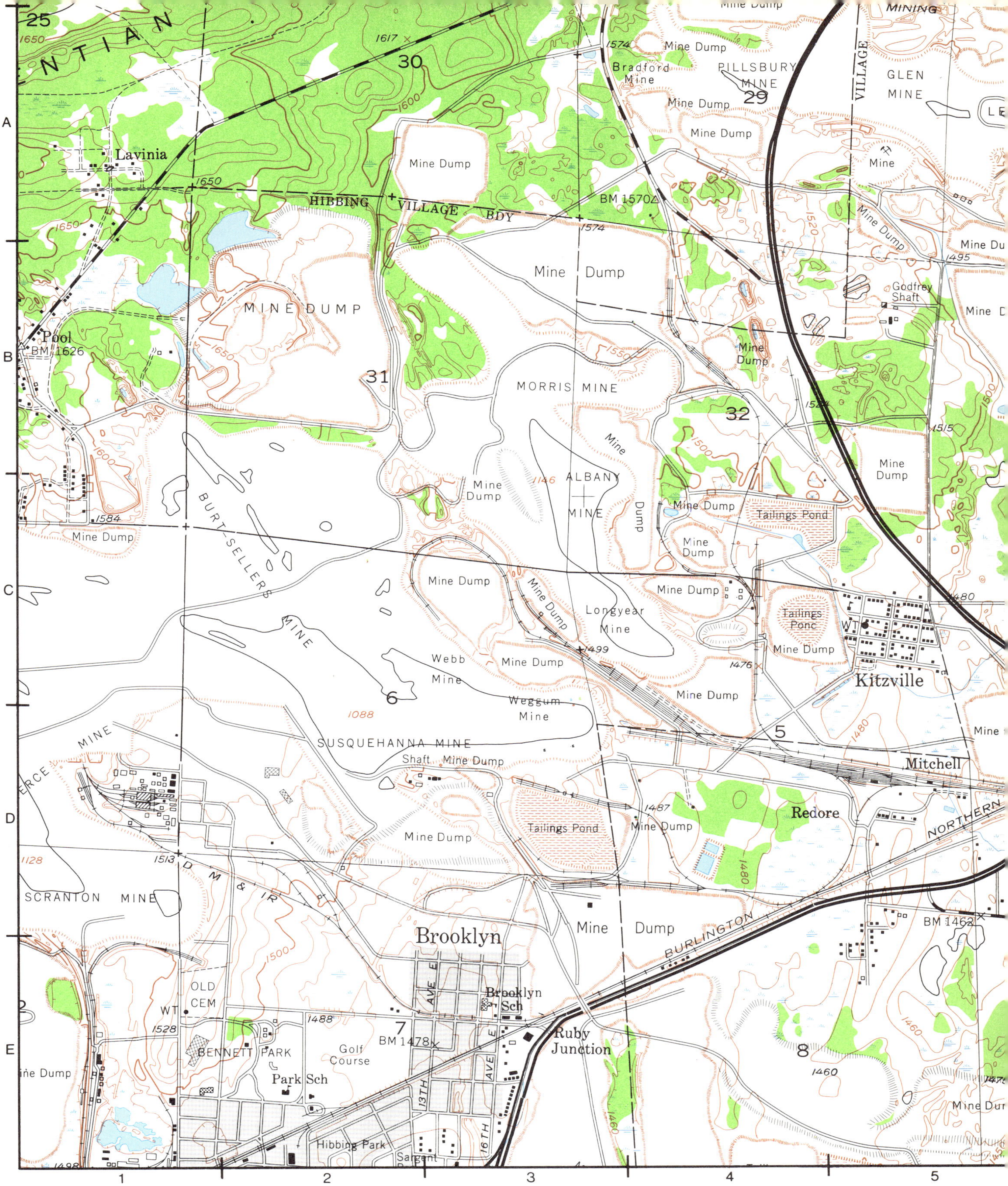

from Hibbing Quadrangle, Minnesota—St. Louis Co.

Scale 1:24,000
Contour Interval 10 ft.
Latitude 47° 25′ 30″ N to 47° 29′ N
Longitude 92° 53′ 30″ W to 92° 57′ W

1/2 0 1 MILE

1 .5 0 1 KILOMETER

COAL CITY, ILLINOIS

Man's role in changing the face of the earth is nowhere more apparent and more destructive than in strip mining. This map shows an area of strip coal mining in the Eastern Interior Coal Province of eastern Illinois. Mining was begun here in 1875 when underground shafts were employed to obtain the coal. The expenses involved in drilling, tunneling, conveying and ventilating systems, however, became too high and the method of strip mining was adopted.

Coal occurs as beds between layers of other sedimentary rock. Therefore, strip mining is quite simple. A large dragline strips off the soil and mantle overburden and piles the debris to one side on the ground in long, narrow rows. When the coal bed is exposed, power shovels dig out the coal and pile it on trucks or narrow-gauge railroad cars. The coal is then transported to a grading plant, and from there to market. When the entire coal bed is removed, the dragline begins another strip. The effects of coal mining dominate the map. Names such as Carbon Hill and Coal City suggest the importance of coal to the area.

Vegetation is not easily reestablished on a mined surface, because the surface is made up of unweathered materials and because of the acidity that comes from its association with coal. The windrows of overburden, devoid of vegetation, are exposed to the erosive effects of rain and surface runoff and are further destroyed by gullying and sheetwash. Lakes and ponds form in the unfilled furrows.

1. Why is strip mining preferred over shaft mining?
2. Name the cultural features associated with mining that can be seen on the map and photograph.
3. Have mining operations caused more destruction in Coal City, Illinois, or Bingham Canyon, Utah?
4. Why has man attempted to reestablish vegetation on the mined areas? Why is vegetation denser on some mined areas than on others?
5. Which area in the photograph appears to be mined most recently?
6. Other than the survey lines on the map, what other evidences of the Public Land Survey can be seen in this area?
7. Why did mining operations not molest the cemetery near Dell Abbey?
8. What natural conditions are necessary for strip mining to be carried out in an area? Under what conditions would shaft mining be used?

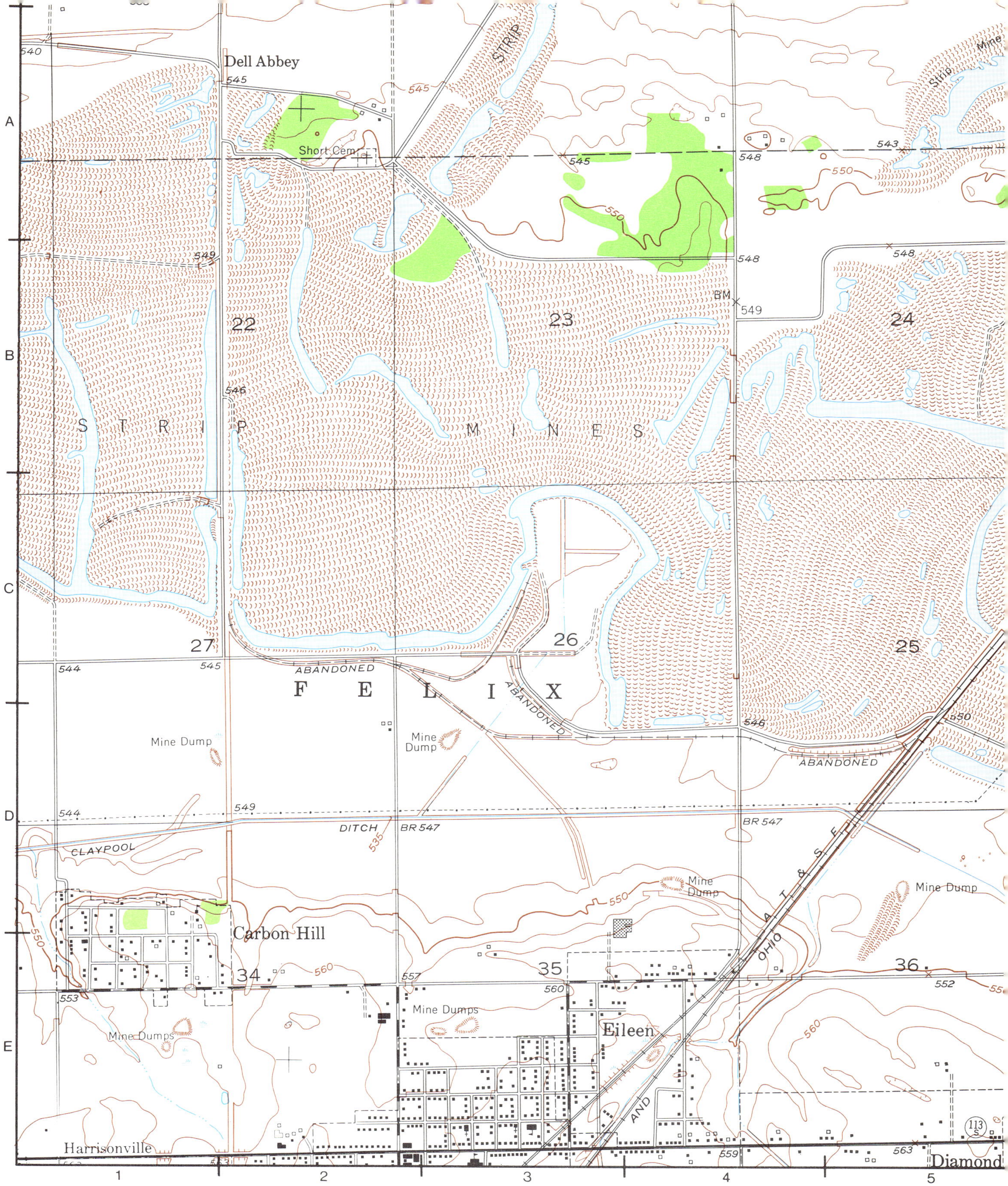

from Coal City Quadrangle, Illinois – Grundy Co.

1/2 0 1 MILE

1 .5 0 1 KILOMETER

Scale 1:24,000
Contour Interval 5 ft.
Latitude 41° 17′ N to 41° 20′ 30″ N
Longitude 88° 15′ W to 88° 11′ 30″ W

ROCK ISLAND DAM, WASHINGTON

The Rock Island Dam was the first dam built on the Columbia River. Most Columbia River dams provide not only electricity to nearby communities but also irrigation water. The Rock Island Dam, however, only generates electricity because it is located too far from potentially irrigable lands and has a storage capacity too small for flood control.

The Rock Island Dam, which is about 3,800 feet long, is built of reinforced concrete; its base is set in the bedrock under the river. It impounds a reservoir 23 miles long and about 3,000 acres in extent. It has numerous spillways and fish ladders. Ten hydroelectric turbines generate a total of 250,000 kilowatts. The penstocks, large pipes that carry water from the reservoir to the powerhouse, are buried in the concrete structure. In a dam such as the Rock Island Dam, the generation of electricity depends on the drop of water from the reservoir to the stream level below to supply the force to turn the generators. Transmission lines carry current from the Rock Island Dam to nearby substations.

1. Describe the settlement pattern in this area. To what is it oriented?
2. Describe the vegetation in this area. What evidences of agriculture can be seen?
3. How do the survey lines indicate the difficulties of surveying in a rough topographic area?
4. Identify the fish ladder, powerhouse and power transmission lines on the photograph with the help of the map. For what is each used?
5. Identify the structure on the west bank of the reservoir. Explain its use.
6. By use of the map and photograph, determine the height of the dam.

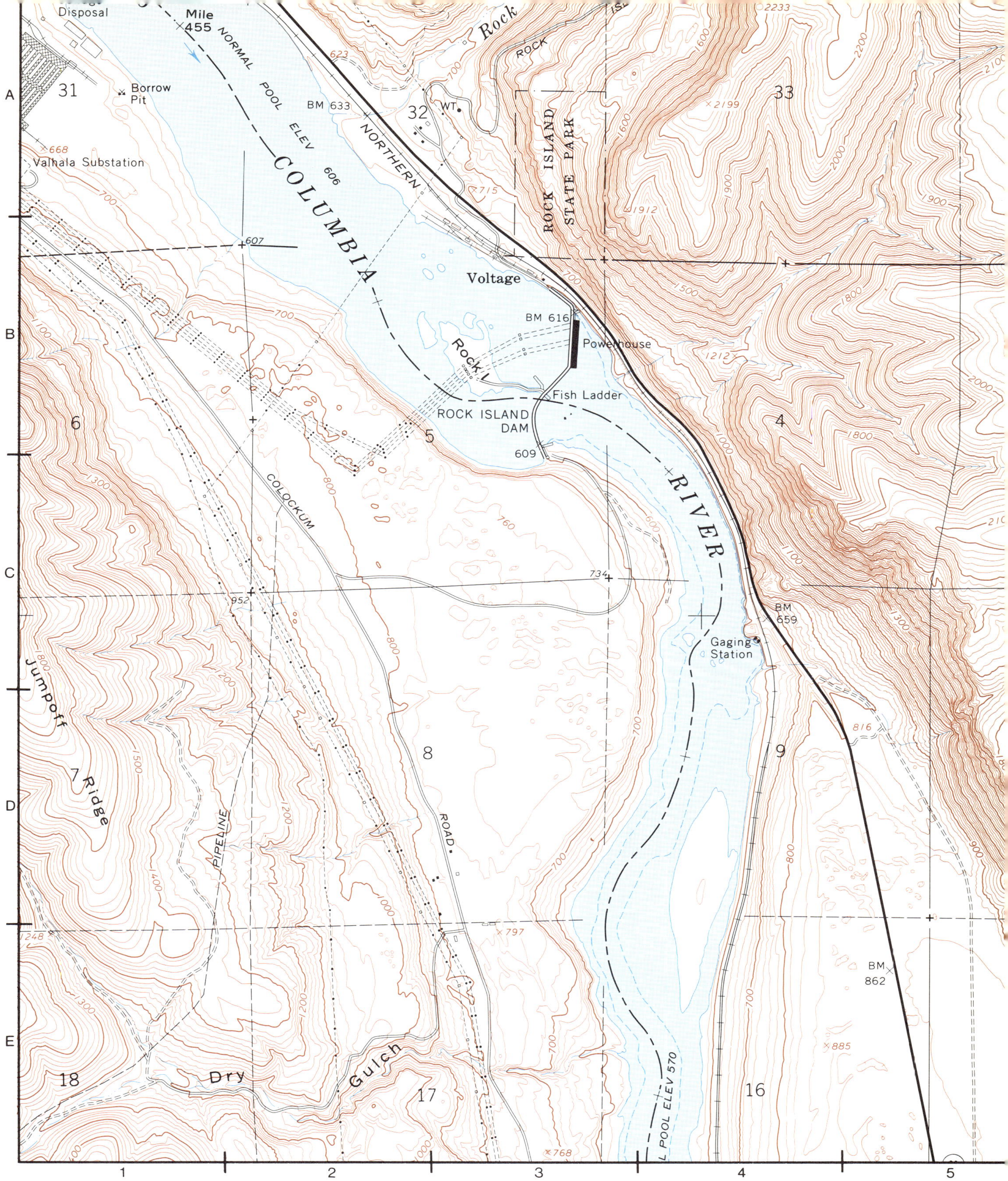

from Rock Island Dam Quadrangle, Washington

Scale 1:24,000
Contour Interval 20 ft.
Latitude 47° 18′ 30″ N to 47° 21′ 30″ N
Longitude 120° 03′ 30″ W to 120° 07′ 30″ W

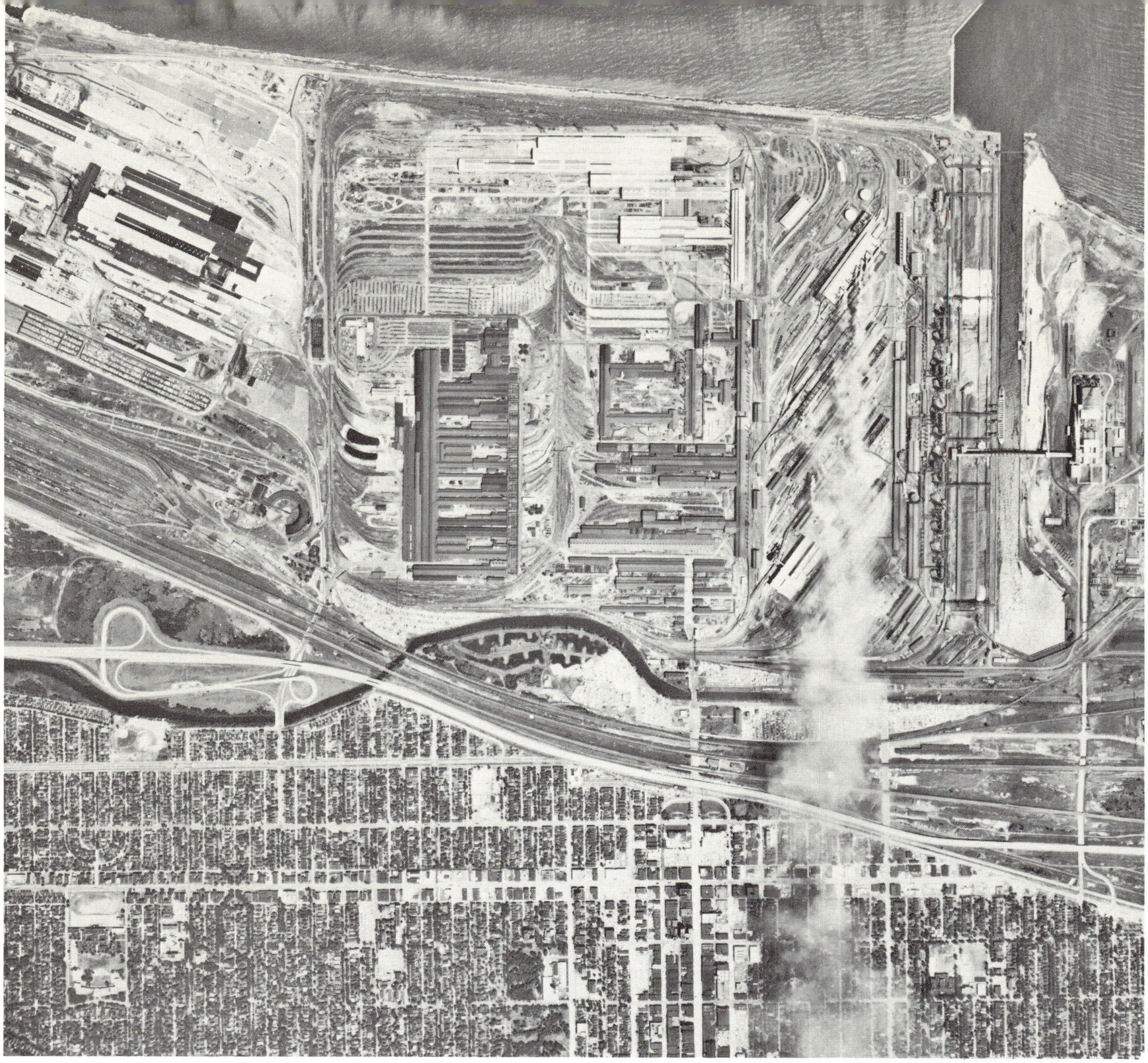

GARY, INDIANA

This part of the Calumet region is located on Lake Michigan north of the Valparaiso Moraine. Formerly it was an area of sand ridges alternating with swamps, but its potential lay in its location between the iron-producing regions of the Lake Superior District to the northwest and the coal and limestone deposits to the southeast.

The city of Gary and the massive industrial area along the southern shore of Lake Michigan were created by the United States Steel Corporation. In 1906 Judge Elbert H. Gary, chairman of the board of U.S. Steel Corporation, bought thousands of acres along Lake Michigan. The steel mills were soon built and the city of Gary was platted around them. The blast furnaces produced their first steel in 1909. Since then smaller industries manufacturing steel springs, screws, bolts, tubing, cement, hosiery, chemicals, and soap products have gravitated to Gary.

North of Gary, across the Calumet River, is the Carnegie-Illinois Steel plant. Many aspects of steel production can be identified on the map and the aerial photograph. Most observable are the steel mills, blast furnaces, slag dumps, iron ore stockpiles, powerhouses and water-cooling devices, along with a variety of other shops and buildings.

Although Gary was a planned city, the street pattern and urban arrangement are not particularly conducive to smooth traffic flow. By and large, the street and road pattern in the area correspond to the section lines of the Public Land Survey.

1. Why did the chemical industries and industries that manufacture products of iron and steel locate in this area?
2. What is the use of the coke ovens? Locate them on the aerial photograph.
3. What features identify the blast furnace? What is the use of the shuttle-car that runs to the top of the blast furnace?
4. Which roads correspond to the survey lines and which do not? Explain the differences.
5. Why are railroad routes not oriented to the survey lines? (Refer to maps in other sections.)
6. Is the industry well served by transportation facilities? How?
7. Both Duisburg, West Germany, and Gary, Indiana, are major steel manufacturing areas. What do they have in common? How do they differ?

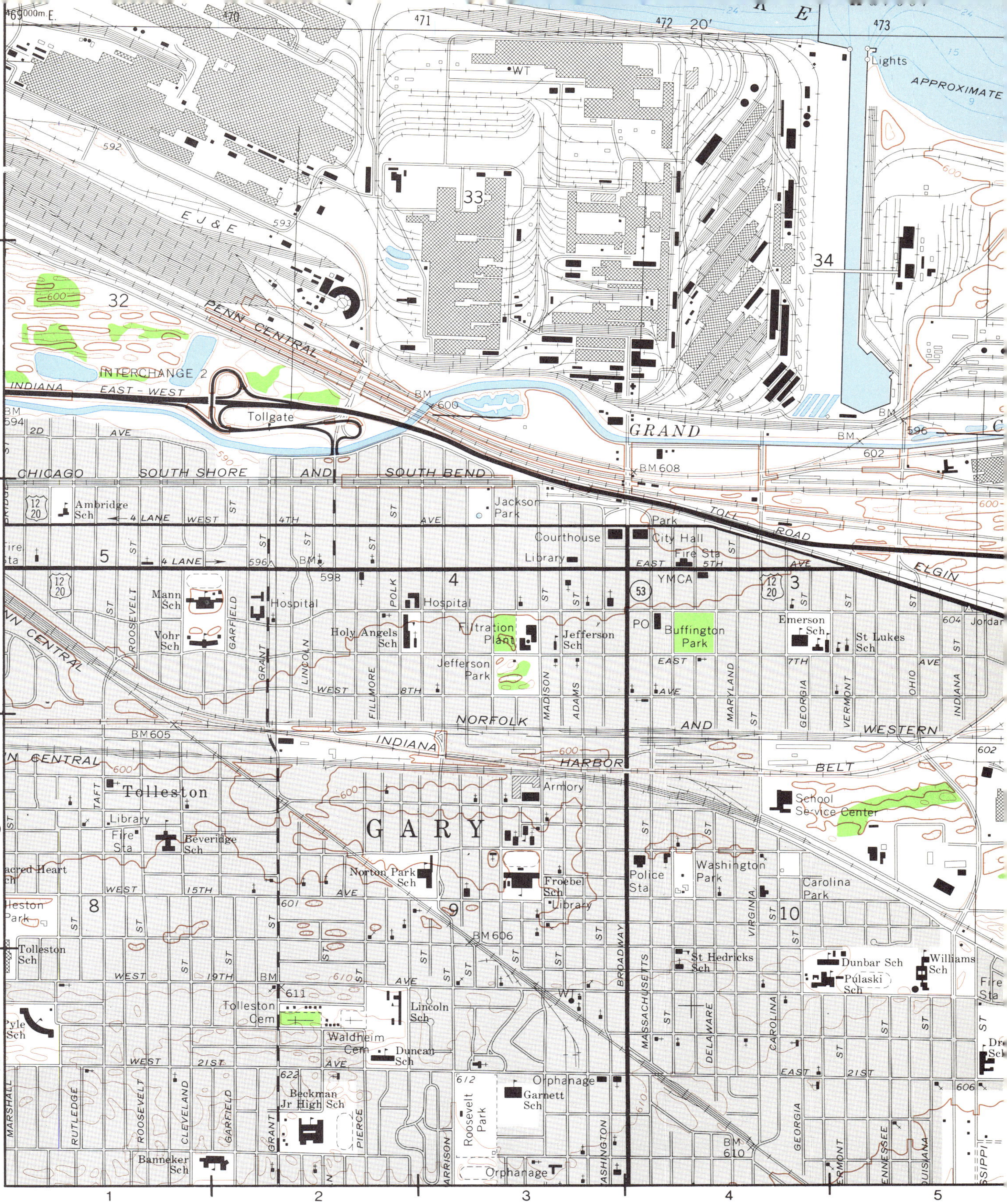

from Gary Quadrangle, Indiana—Lake Co.

Scale 1:24,000
Contour Interval 10 ft.
Latitude 41° 34′ 30″ N to 41° 37′ 30″ N
Longitude 87° 19′ W to 87° 22′ 30″ W

DUISBURG, WEST GERMANY

Duisburg, located in the Rhineland-Westphalian region of West Germany at the confluence of the Rhine and Ruhr rivers, is noted for its iron and steel industry as well as for its excellent harbor facilities. Duisburg is one of the largest inland ports in the world, being connected to the North Sea by the Rhine River and the Rhine-Herne Canal.

The main section of the city lies to the south of the Ruhr River. An attractive business district gives way on the south and east to suburbs that spread into the surrounding hills, some of which are still clothed with a mixed forest of deciduous and pine trees. The street pattern is as erratic in the suburbs as it is in the city itself.

Duisburg received heavy damage from Allied bombings during World War II. Many of the ancient buildings were destroyed, and modern city planning has created an attractive, functional urban area. The bridges across the Rhine have been rebuilt since the war. Broad streets and modern buildings characterize that section of the city south of the Ruhr River, but the area near the Rhine and Ruhr rivers is a smoke-filled industrial complex, dominated by heavy-lift cranes and piles of coal and chemicals.

Duisburg holds special interest for the geographer because it was here that Mercator did much of his work. He is buried in the Salvatorkirche and the opera hall is named in his honor. A Mercator museum is located in Duisburg where the original Mercator celestial sphere and world chart are on display.

1. In what ways does Duisburg differ from an industrial American city?
2. Where is most of the heavy industry concentrated? Why?
3. Where is the port section of the city located? Identify the docks, the railroad tracks, the marshalling yards and the oil tank farms (Olinsel).
4. What are the canals used for?
5. What type of vegetation can be identified in this area?
6. Compare the symbols used on this map with those used on United States quadrangles. Explain the differences and similarities.

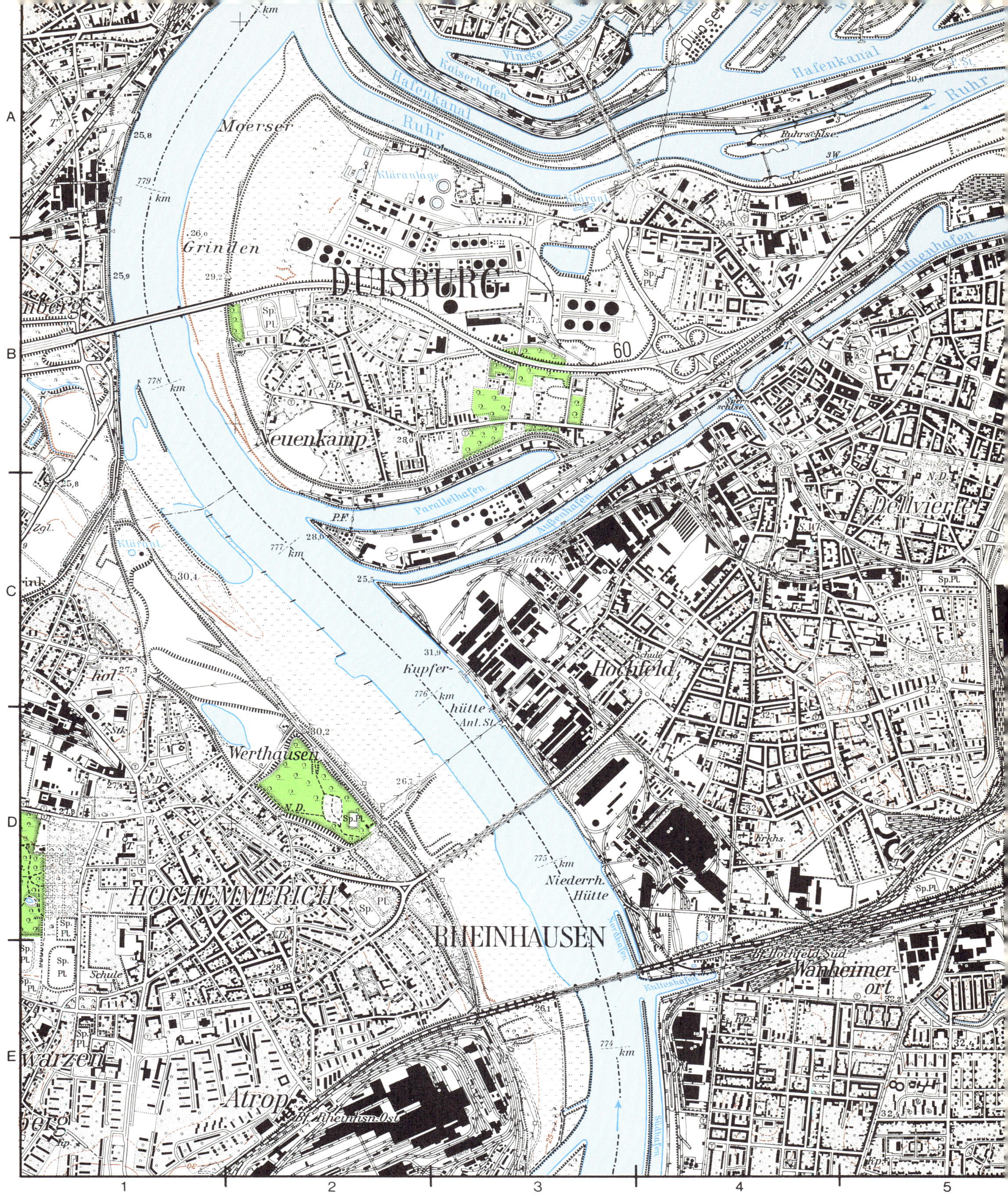

from Duisburg, West Germany

Reproduced through the courtesy of
Landesvermessungsamtes, Nordrhein-Westfalen, West Germany

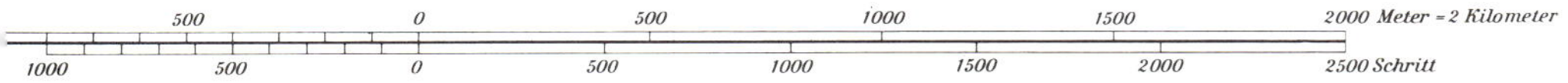

Scale	1:25,000 (cm.)
Contour Interval	20 m.
Latitude	51° 24′ N to 51° 27′ N
Longitude	6° 42′ E to 6° 46′ E

KEELER, CALIFORNIA

This map represents an almost uninhabited section between Owens Lake and the Inyo Mountains in the Basin and Range Physiographic Province of California. The depression of Owens Lake, which was formed during the Pleistocene Epoch, was filled by meltwaters from the glaciers in the Sierra Nevada Mountains. Once the glaciers had receded the water evaporated under the dry climate, and at present only a playa remains. The beach ridges that remained as the water shrank away from the shore can be detected on both the map and the aerial photograph.

The only sources of water are underground springs, but the streams that emerge from them dry out within a short distance of the springs. The streams in the Inyo Mountains that rim the playa are intermittent, and few reach the playa bed. Those that do end in intermittent saline pools. Pipelines carry the salt-charged waters from wells in Owens Lake to evaporating pans in and around Keeler. Soda evaporators and a soda-ash product plant are located southeast of Keeler. Also, borax is extracted from Owens Lake.

1. What use is made of the footpath that runs along the pipeline toward the center of the playa?
2. Describe the street pattern of Keeler.
3. What use is made of soda ash and borax?
4. Why do the streams in the southwest corner of the map end abruptly?
5. Describe the Public Land Survey system on the map.
6. What cultural features can be identified in the mountains on the eastern part of the map? What is the upper elevation of cultural features in this area?
7. Describe the climate in this area. From the aerial photograph, describe the type and distribution of vegetation.

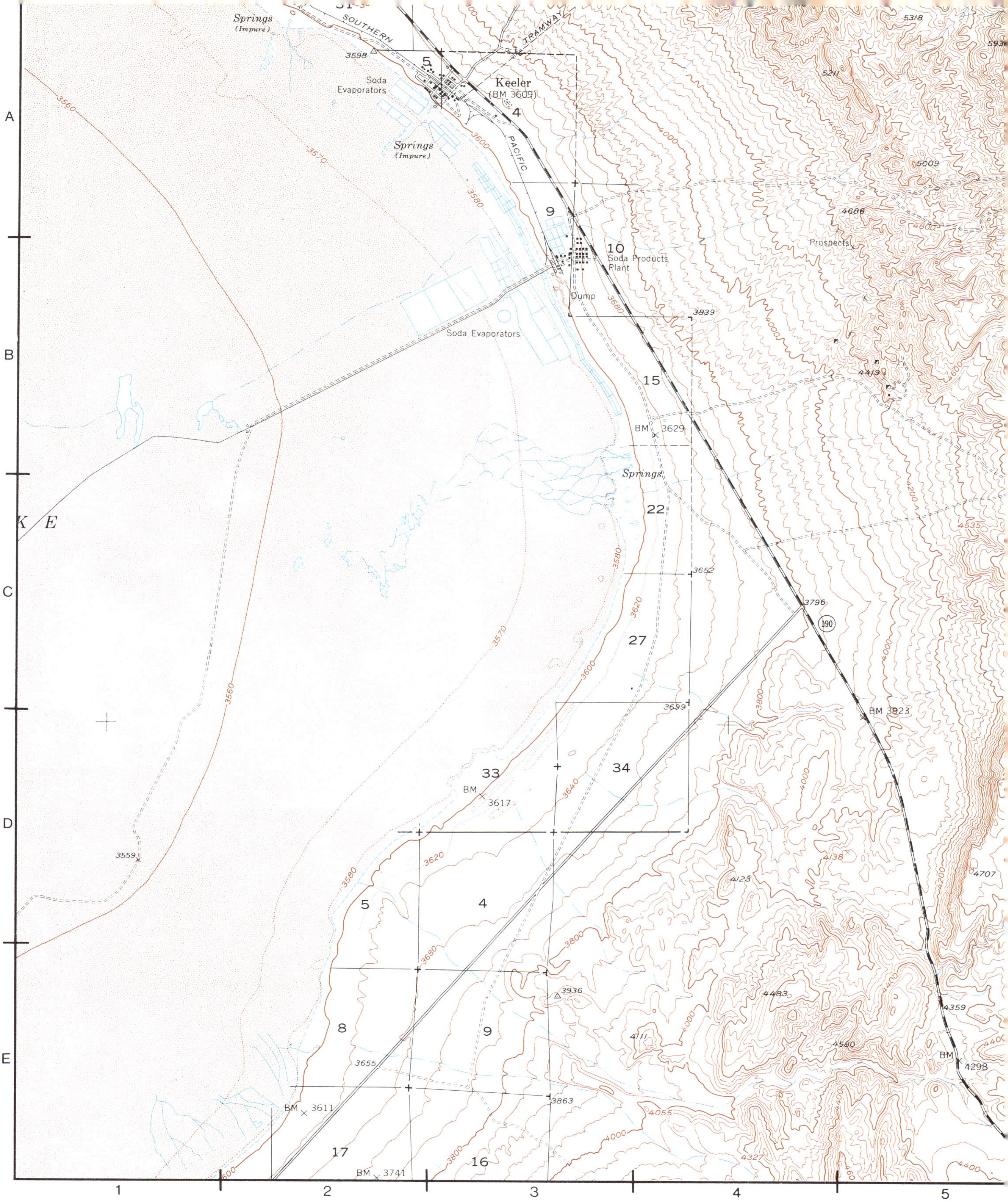

from Keeler Quadrangle, California—Inyo Co.

Scale 1:62,500
Contour Interval 40 ft.
Latitude 36° 22′ N
to 36° 30′ N
Longitude 117° 47′ 30″ W
to 117° 55′ 30″ W

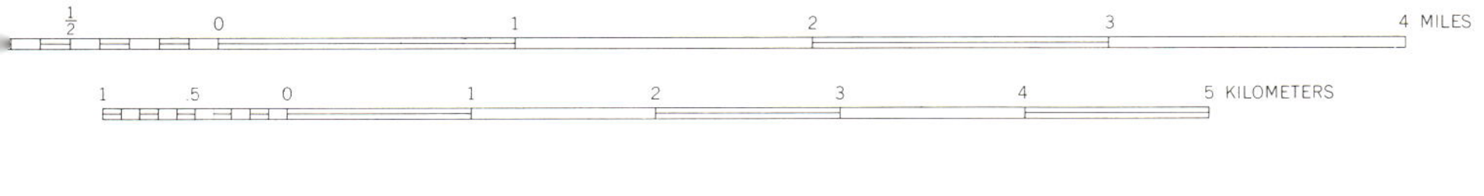

Transportation Impressions

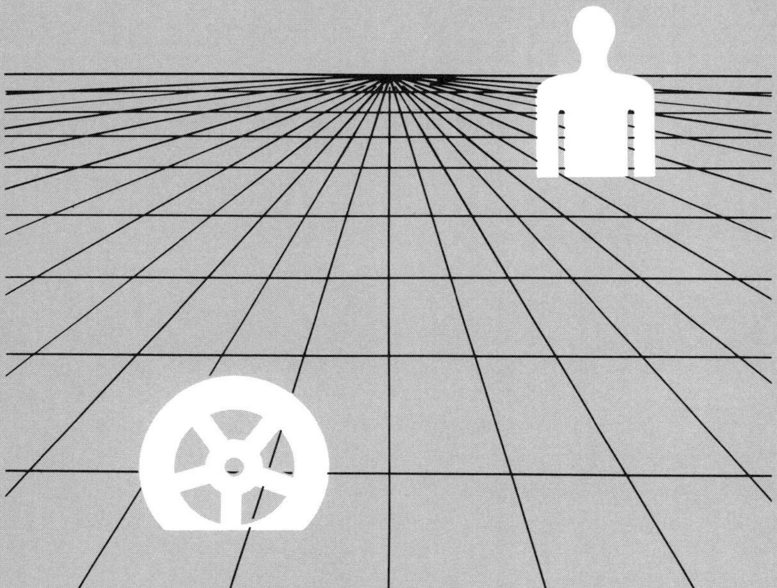

The settlement of the United States progressed mostly along the lines of easy access to the interior. The early transportation routes followed rivers and lakes or animal and Indian trails.

The first roads were built to transport troops and settlers to the interior and to carry farm produce back to the coast. They followed river valleys or ridgetops and took advantage of water gaps through the mountains. By 1775, post roads and stage roads had been built along the Eastern Seaboard. In the 1780's a number of routes crossed the Appalachian highlands. Settlement not only expanded into the interior but along these routes themselves, as well as into the valleys they followed. The turnpike boom began in the 1790's. New roads were built and existing roads were improved; some were even paved. Bridges were built and toll stations were established.

Today, many modern superhighways closely follow the same routes as the pioneer roads. The modern highways have limited access and intersect each other by means of complex interchanges.

In addition to the modern highways, rural roads lace the countryside. In some parts of the midwest, the rural roads follow the section lines of the Public Land Survey, forming a gridlike pattern. In those areas where settlement preceded the survey, the roads may follow ridgetops or valleys, or they may illustrate no particular orientation. As engineering skills improved, many roads were straightened and relocated.

The return to water transportation occurred during the canal-building era that began with the Erie Canal in 1825. By 1850, more than 4,000 miles of canals had been constructed. Waterways permit bulk transportation for a comparatively cheap price. Natural waterways, supplemented in places by canals, extend from the heart of the nation to the Atlantic coast. By way of these waterways, oceangoing steamers can reach the ports on the Great Lakes. Associated with these ports are cargo warehouses, loading cranes, docks, slips, drawbridges, locks, navigation lights, buoy locations, channel markers and even exposed wrecks.

Railroads began to expand in the early part of the nineteenth century. In 1830, there were only 23 miles of railroads in the country, but within 50 years more than 93,000 miles of railroads went into operation. Although in recent years passenger traffic has declined, railroads still carry a large amount of freight.

The major form of passenger transportation today, after the automobile, is the airplane. Numerous airports with their paved runways and terminals have recently been added to the cultural landscape.

The methods by which energy, voice and pictures are transported can be seen on topographic maps. Power lines, radio towers, television relay stations, and telephone cables and pipelines are a part of the cultural landscape in many areas.

Roads, canals, railroads and air traffic have greatly influenced industrial development, which, in turn, has caused transportation to expand. The growth of the industrial complex in the United States has demanded not only more roads and railroad lines but also numerous associated structures, such as switching yards, terminals and docking facilities. They are as much a part of industry as of transportation.

DUNCANNON, PENNSYLVANIA

Duncannon is an important point on one of the historic westward routes through the Appalachian highlands. Westward movement from the Atlantic Seaboard was obstructed by the Appalachian highlands. Since the time of early settlement, travelers had to take advantage of the valleys and the numerous watergaps through the ridges. One of the early routes followed the Susquehanna River to its junction of the Juniata River where Duncannon is located. It then followed the Juniata valley through successive ridges to the Allegheny Front near Altoona. On the west side of the Front, the route followed the headwaters of the Allegheny River, to the forks of the Ohio River at Pittsburgh, where the Ohio Valley provided access to the interior. This route was used from about 1780 onward by fur traders and some settlers. Today, many of the major east-west routes follow the same course.

The only major settlement in this area is Duncannon. Its street pattern is oriented mainly along the Susquehanna River, indicating the former importance of water transportation.

Agriculture is mostly confined to dairying, since cultivation is limited by the mountainous terrain.

1. What function did Duncannon serve in the days of early settlement?
2. Identify the different kinds of transportation seen on the map and photograph. How are they influenced by the topography?
3. Describe the rural settlement pattern in this area. To what factors does it owe its pattern?
4. On a map of the United States, follow the early pioneer route described above.
5. Describe the distribution of forests in this area. Explain why the hills are not cultivated.
6. What features on the map indicate a change in transportation and the importance of rural communities?
7. Describe the topography of the ridge and valley region.

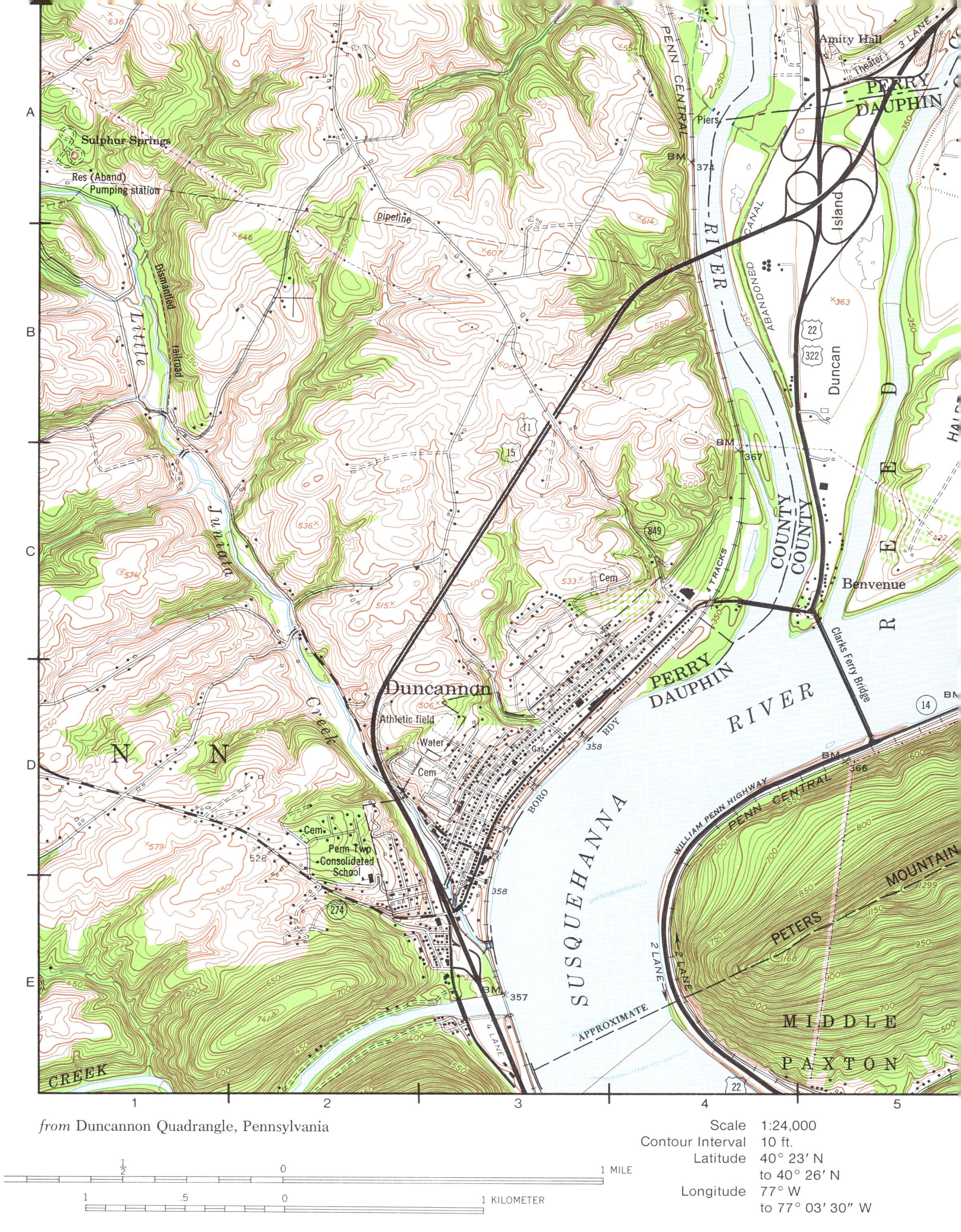

from Duncannon Quadrangle, Pennsylvania

Scale 1:24,000
Contour Interval 10 ft.
Latitude 40° 23′ N to 40° 26′ N
Longitude 77° W to 77° 03′ 30″ W

CUMBERLAND, MARYLAND/PENNSYLVANIA/WEST VIRGINIA

Cumberland, formerly called Wills Creek, was founded by the Ohio Company at the confluence of Wills Creek and the Potomac River in 1750. George Washington built the first fort at Wills Creek in 1754 as a defense against French and Indian attacks. In spite of its location in the heart of the mountain wilderness, Cumberland grew because of its proximity to several major westward routes and local resources.

The Potomac River, on which Cumberland is located, was one of the easiest and most popular routes from the east coast to the interior. Braddock's Road, from Baltimore to Pittsburgh, provided access westward. The road was built in 1755 to transport Braddock's army from Cumberland to Ft. Duquesne near Pittsburgh. Another route that increased the importance of Cumberland was the National Road, also known as the Cumberland Road or the "Pike." It is now U.S. 40. The road was 66 feet wide, and partially macadamized, which made it one of the finest roads of its time. It began at Cumberland where it met the Fredrick Pike from Baltimore. From there it continued to Illinois. Transportation to the west was improved even further when the Chesapeake & Ohio Canal and the Baltimore & Ohio Railroad were built. Today, the major avenue of transportation is U.S. 40, which follows Wills Creek through the Narrows.

1. Identify the transportation routes described above.
2. Describe the settlement pattern along U.S. 40.
3. Why is the settlement pattern better developed along U.S. 40 than along any other highway on the map?
4. How can new urban subdivisions be identified? Where are they located?
5. Describe and account for the settlement patterns in the valleys.
6. Describe the natural vegetation of this region.
7. Compare the map of Cumberland Gap with that of Middlesboro South, Tennessee. List the similarities. Compare Cumberland with Cumberland Gap.

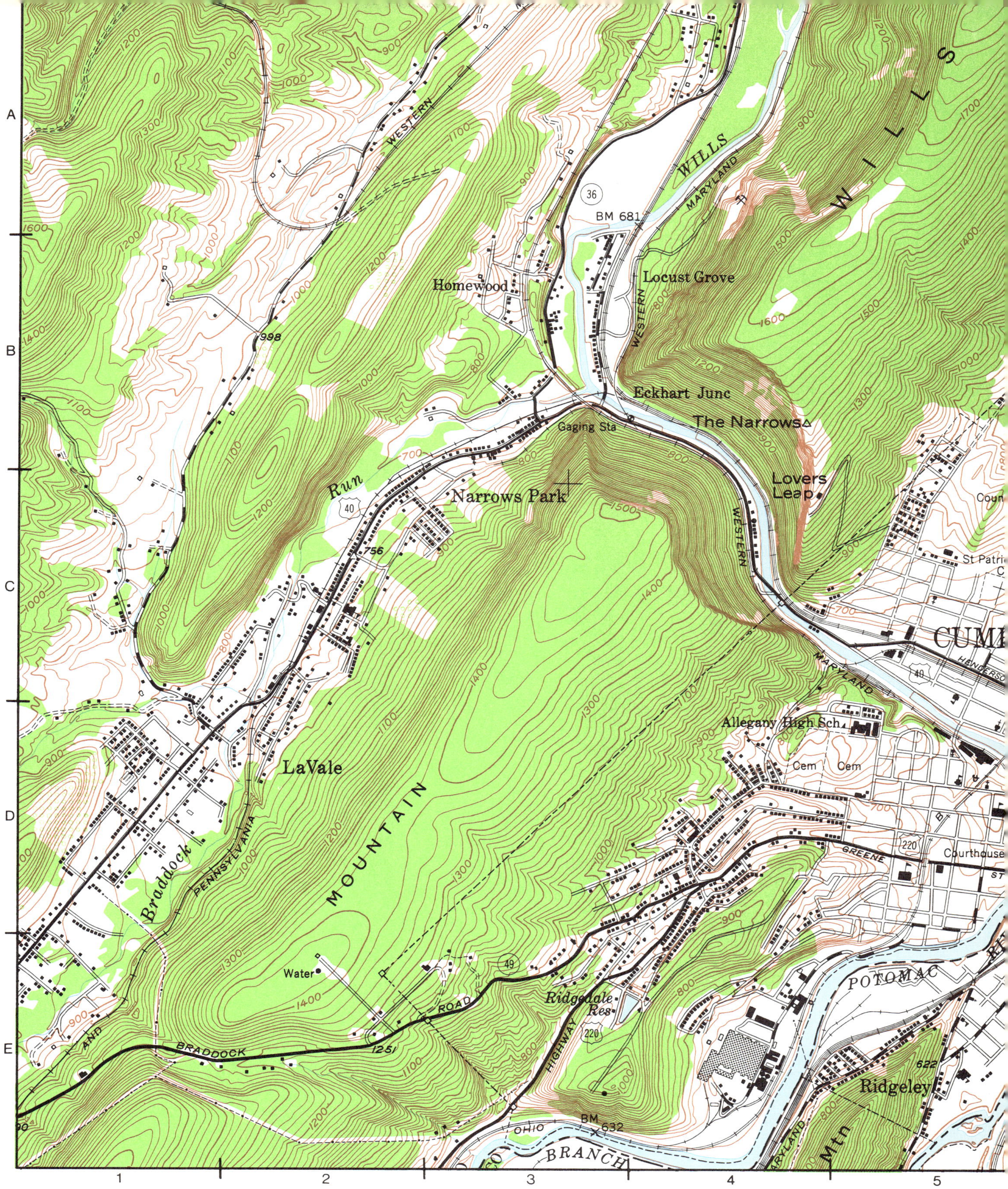

from Cumberland Quadrangle, Maryland/Pennsylvania/West Virginia

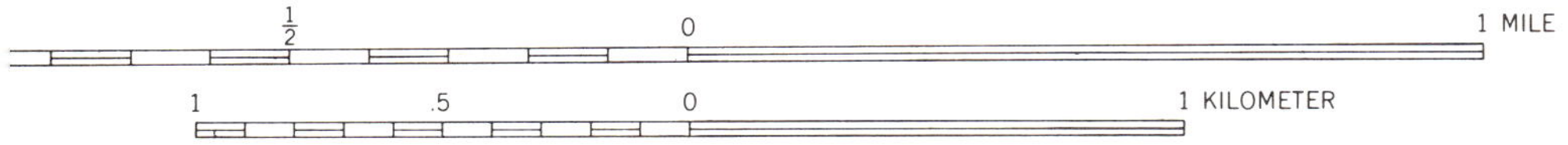

Scale 1:24,000
Contour Interval 20 ft.
Latitude 39° 38′ N to 39° 41′ 30″ N
Longitude 78° 46′ W to 78° 49′ 30″ W

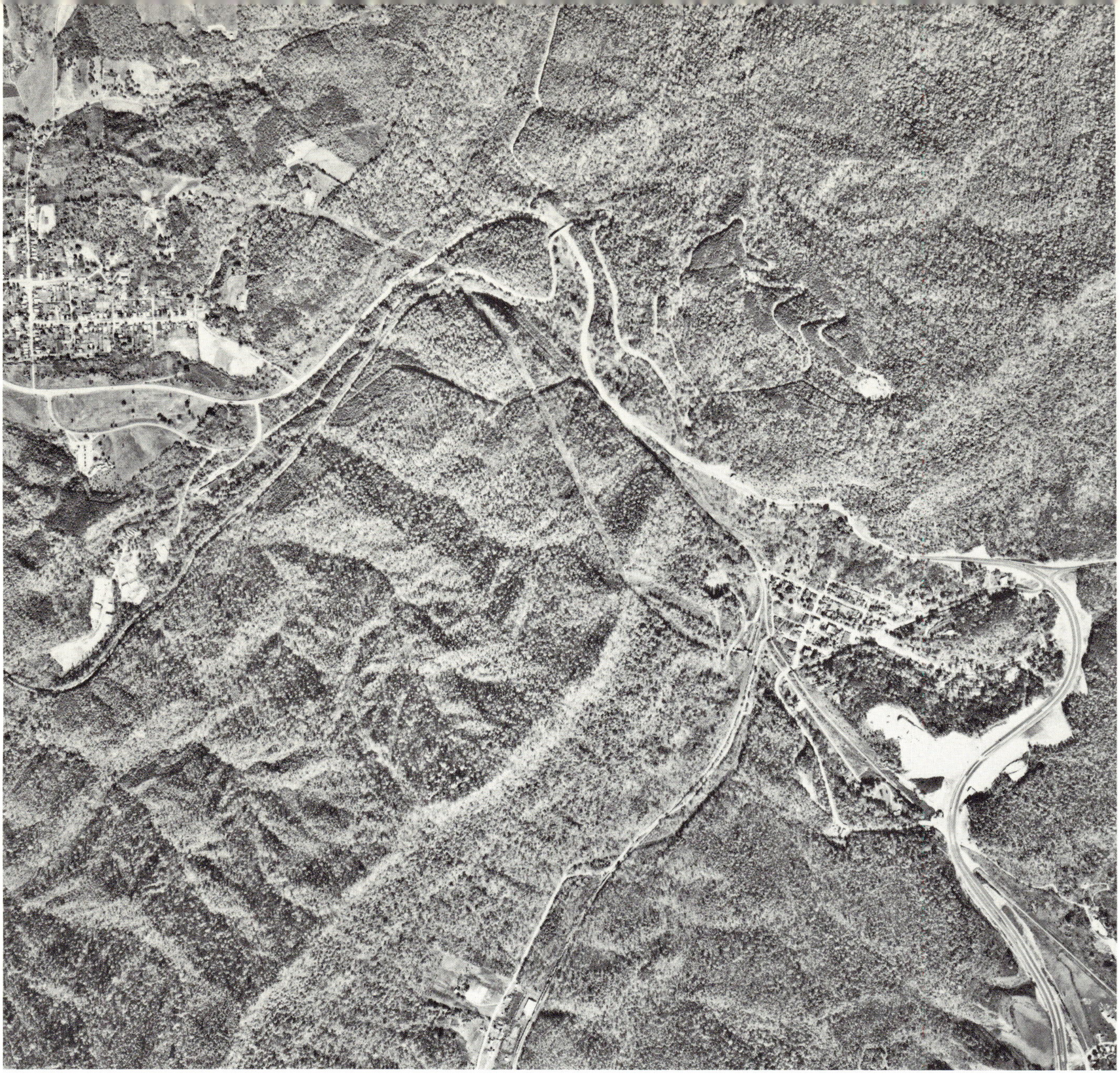

MIDDLESBORO SOUTH, TENNESSEE/KENTUCKY/VIRGINIA

The Cumberland Gap was the most frequented corridor through the Appalachian barrier. The routes through Pennsylvania were difficult and other avenues farther north and south were blocked by hostile Indians. The most popular immigrant route was the Wilderness Road that led from the Shenandoah Valley through the Cumberland Gap to the Bluegrass Basin and the lower Ohio Valley. The route through the gap was previously used by Cherokee and Shawnee Indian hunters and was called "Warrior's Path."

The first European to discover it was Dr. Thomas Walker of the Loyal Land Grant Company of Virginia. The route through the gap, however, was not used for several years because of the Indian Wars. The first trail through the gap was blazed by Daniel Boone in 1773, following which time the first settlement of Transylvania was established at its western end, south of the Kentucky River. In 1792, the Wilderness Road was widened to accommodate wagons, but the defeat of the Indians in the north and the development of more direct westward routes reduced the stream of immigrants through the gap.

Today the same route is used, but the old trail is replaced by the concrete lanes of the modern Dixie Highway (U.S. 25E). The Louisville and Nashville Railroad also uses this route, and other communication lines, such as a power line and a telephone line, follow the gap.

1. What early trans-Appalachian routes are followed by major east-west roads or railroads?
2. How does the railroad cross the gap?
3. Account for the shape and pattern of the city of Cumberland Gap.
4. Identify the cultural features other than settlements on the map.
5. Describe the distribution of forests in this area.
6. Compare the vegetation to that seen on the aerial photographs of East Portal, Colorado.

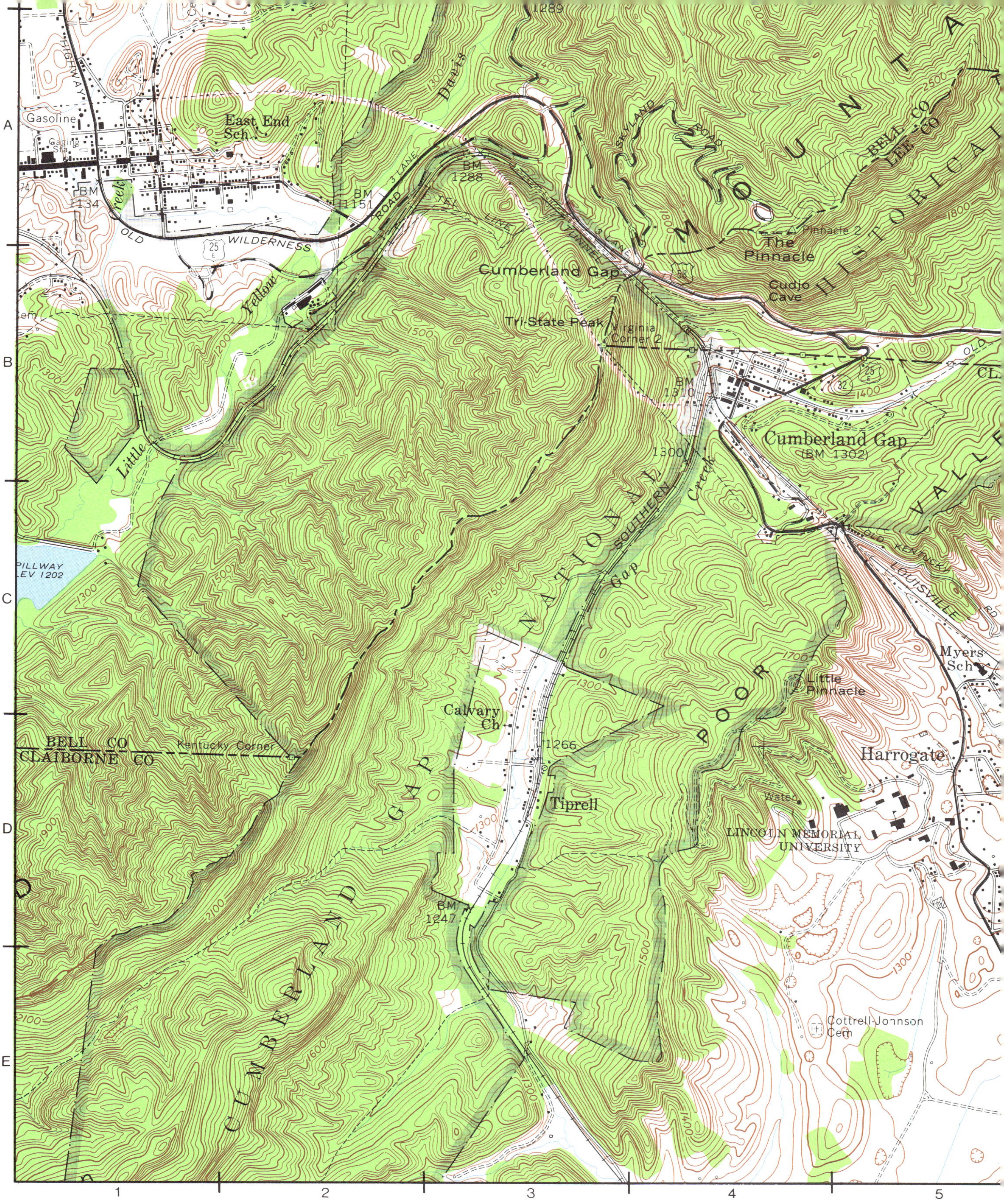

from Middlesboro South Quadrangle, Tennessee/Kentucky/Virginia

Scale 1:24,000
Contour Interval 20 ft.
Latitude 36° 34′ N to 36° 37′ N
Longitude 83° 39′ 30″ W to 83° 42′ 30″ W

½ 0 1 MILE

1 .5 0 1 KILOMETER

SCOTTSBLUFF, NEBRASKA

When westward migration across the Great Plains began, the major task was the exploration and establishment of the easiest routes. Several trails were established across the Great Plains toward the west coast. Although the trails were several miles apart, they converged to take advantage of a pass or a river valley through a ridge.

Mitchell Pass, Nebraska, through the highland of Scottsbluff was one of them. The bluff was one of the signal and lookout points along the Oregon Trail. The Oregon Trail to the northwest, the Pony Express Route and the Overland Trail to California all crossed through Mitchell Pass. The Mormon Trail ran a short distance away, north of the North Platte River.

Both the Oregon Trail and the Mormon Trail carried thousands of emigrants to the intermontane basins and the Willamette Valley in Oregon. The Oregon Trail was probably blazed in the 1800's by trappers whose destination was Astoria on the west coast. The great migration of settlers, however, did not begin until the early 1840's. Some settlers traveled in wagon trains, or on horseback with pack animals carrying their belongings. Others walked, pushing all they possessed in baby carriages and carts, as they trudged to the California gold fields or to their new homes in the west.

1. Why did most of the early migrants find the route through Mitchell Pass easier than the route along the North Platte River?
2. From the map, what indicates that the highland area was used as a signal and lookout point?
3. Is Scottsbluff a likely tourist spot? Explain.
4. What is the purpose of the road that runs from Nebraska 92 to the top of Scotts Bluff?
5. For what purpose is the Gering Canal used?
6. Explain the pattern of the rural roads. Explain the street patterns in the new urban subdivisions in the upper right corner of the map.
7. Explain the origin of the isolated highland of Scotts Bluff. What landform feature is located between Scotts Bluff and the Platte River?

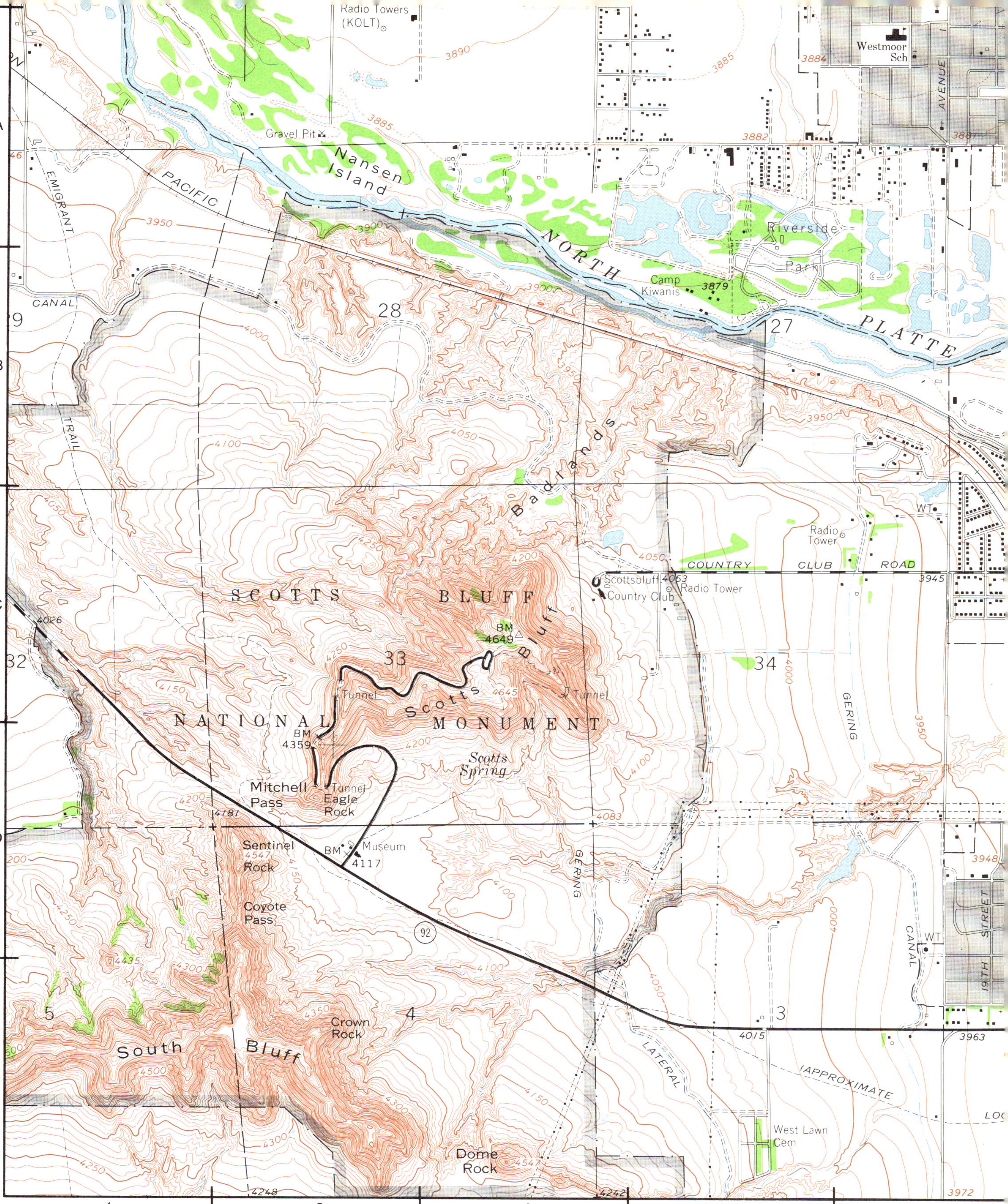

from Scottsbluff South Quadrangle, Nebraska—Scotts Bluff Co.

Scale	1:24,000
Contour Interval	10 ft.
Latitude	41° 48′ 30″ N to 41° 51′ 30″ N
Longitude	103° 40′ W to 103° 43′ 30″ W

EAST PORTAL, COLORADO

East Portal marks one end of a major transportation route through the Rocky Mountains of Colorado. The mountains in this area presented an imposing barrier to westward migration just as the Appalachians did in the east. See Duncannon, Pennsylvania, p. 62; Cumberland, Maryland, p. 64. In the east, the best westward routes followed the river valleys on the eastern side to the divide and the valleys on the western side to the plains. In the southern Rocky Mountains a few passes were in use between headwaters of streams. The mainstream of northern migration crossed the Rockies at South Pass, Wyoming. But similar routes could not be followed across the Colorado Rockies since the divides were too difficult to negotiate. In order to provide a connecting link between Denver and the west coast, an artificial pass was constructed by the Denver and Rio Grande Western Railroad under the Continental Divide. This is the Moffat Tunnel.

The tunnel begins at East Portal and runs through the divide for six miles. The railroad through the Moffat Tunnel is a single standard-gauge track. Double tracks approach the tunnel from both sides and traffic into the tunnel is controlled at both ends.

The tunnel took nearly four years to build. In addition, 38 miles of railroad, called the Dotsero cutoff, were built to connect it to the main line. The cutoff was completed in 1934 at the cost of 3.85 million dollars.

An aqueduct, parallel to the tracks, runs through an 8-foot by 8-foot bore parallel to the train tunnel. The aqueduct provides one of the sources of domestic, industrial and agricultural water for Denver and surrounding areas.

1. What is the major occupation of the people of East Portal?
2. Account for the absence of other settlements in the region.
3. Why is traffic control necessary at both ends of the tunnel?
4. Why must water be brought from the west side of the Continental Divide to the east side?
5. What feature does the Grand County-Gilpin County line follow?
6. Why are there no major roads in the area?

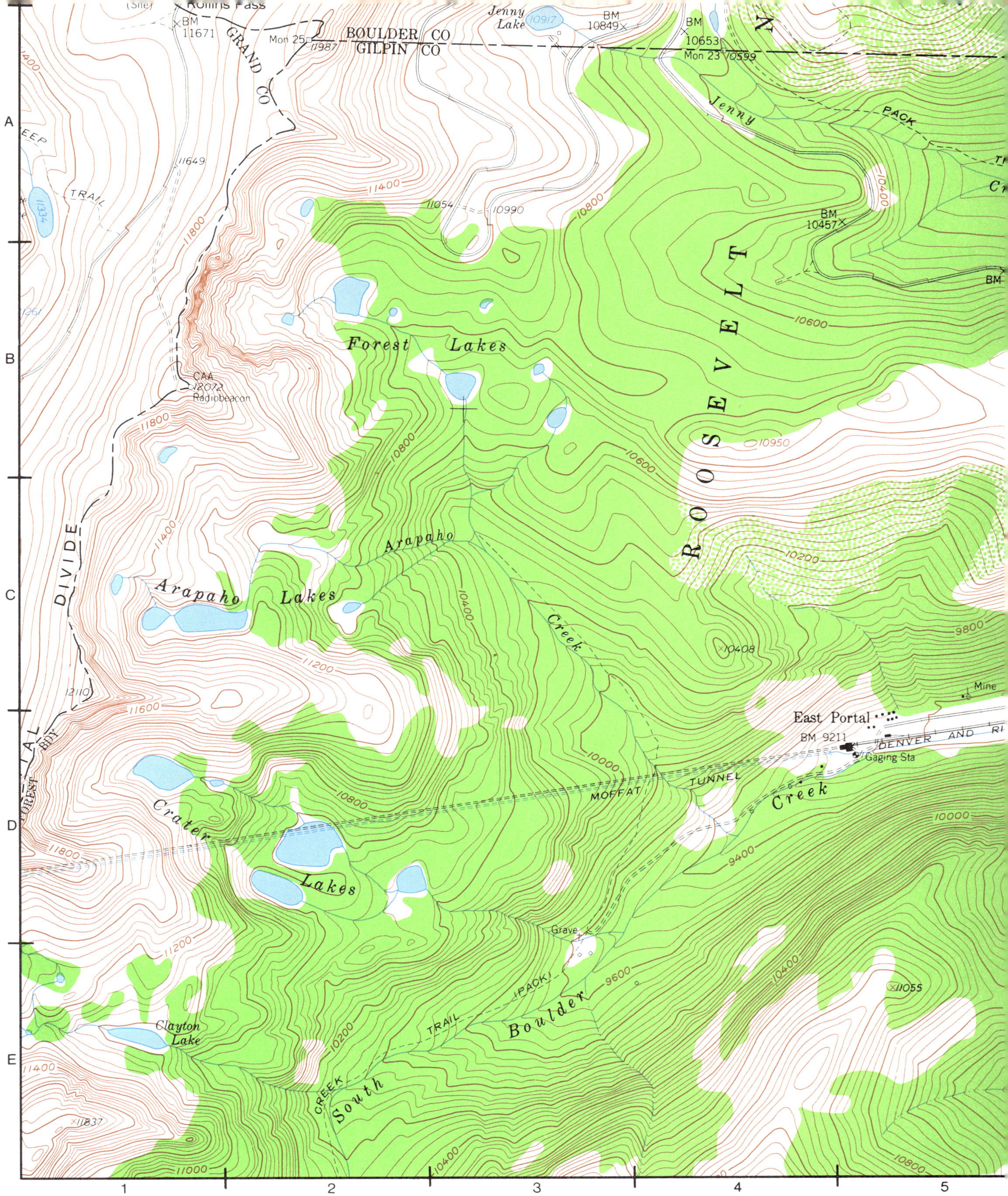

from East Portal Quadrangle, Colorado

Scale	1:24,000
Contour Interval	40 ft.
Latitude	39° 53′ N to 39° 56′ N
Longitude	105° 38′ 30″ W to 105° 41′ 30″ W

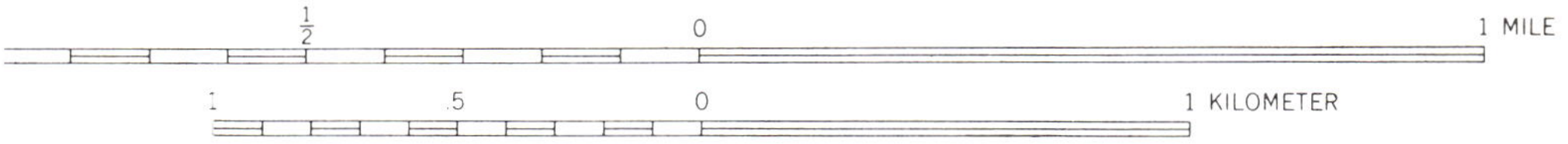

SUPERIOR, WISCONSIN/MINNESOTA

Evidences of all three types of transportation, land, water and air, can be observed on this map and aerial photograph. Before these modern lines of communication were established, however, the area was crossed only by Indian trails.

The area represented by this map was originally Chippewa, Sioux and Ojibway Indian country. Jesuits arrived in the region in the middle of the seventeenth century; however, only minor fur trading posts were established. Permanent settlement in the area did not occur until after the Public Land Survey in 1852.

Although lumbermen and gold-seekers flocked to the area in the 1860's, Duluth did not prosper until 1870 when the tracks of the Northern Pacific Railroad reached the city. Superior assumed importance as a city after iron ore was discovered in Minnesota and shipped through Superior in 1884.

The ports and transportation facilities in and around Duluth and Superior indicate the type of commercial and industrial activities centered in this area. Both cities are ideally located on a natural harbor. St. Louis Bay and Allouez Bay form the harbor, which is protected by sand bars formed by lake currents and waves. The natural entrance to the harbor was between Minnesota Point and Wisconsin Point, but subsequently the entrance at Connors Point was dredged. The largest group of ore docks in the world is located at Allouez, as are some of the longest ore docks (over 2,200 feet). Coal docks are located in the northwestern part of Superior. East of the coal docks is the Great Northern grain elevator. Petroleum storage tank farms and general cargo sheds also can be seen in the area.

The Arrowhead toll bridge connects Superior to Duluth. The ore docks at Duluth are located in the extreme northern part of the map.

1. Explain the railroad pattern in this area.
2. The road pattern in this area is adjusted to two controls. Explain them.
3. Explain the street patterns of Superior, South Superior and Duluth. Contrast these patterns with those of East End, Allouez and Oneota.
4. Explain the location of rural dwellings.
5. Describe the vegetation in this area. Estimate the amount of this area which is under cultivation. Explain.
6. What products other than iron ore are handled by the ports?

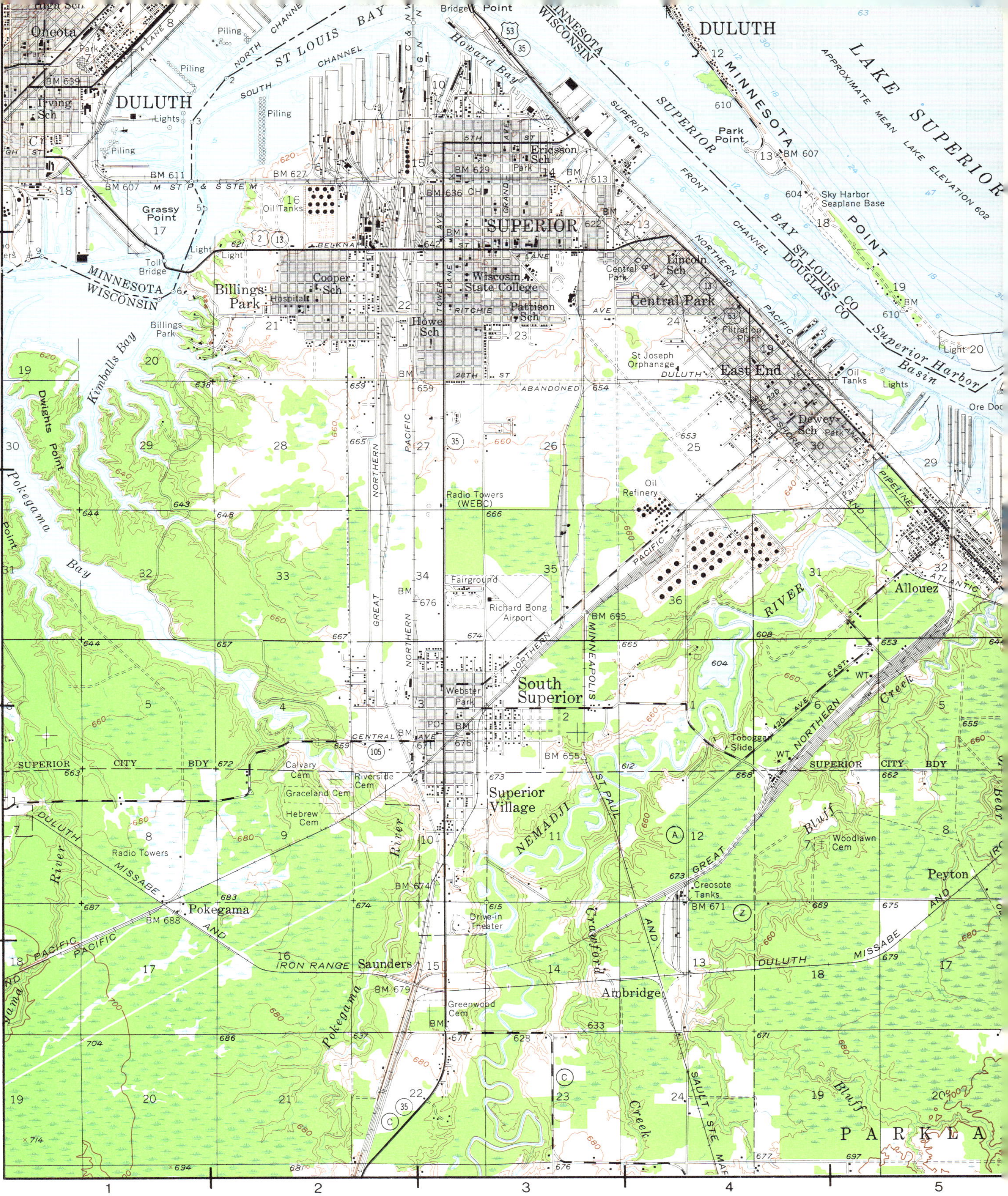

from Superior Quadrangle, Wisconsin/Minnesota

Scale 1:62,500
Contour Interval 20 ft.
Latitude 46° 37′ N to 46° 45′ N
Longitude 92° 00′ 30″ W to 92° 10′ 30″ W

½ 0 1 2 3 4 MILES

1 .5 0 1 2 3 4 5 KILOMETERS

ROMEOVILLE, ILLINOIS

The availability of water transportation is an important factor in the development of industry. The canals seen on the map provide water transportation for the industry of Chicago. Situated on the Great Lakes, Chicago has easy access to both east and west. Cheap water transportation to the south, however, had to be provided.

In 1836–1848 the Illinois–Michigan Canal was built between the headwaters of the Illinois River, which flows into the Mississippi River, and the Chicago River, which flows into Lake Michigan. Thus a continuous water route from Lake Michigan to the Gulf of Mexico, via the Mississippi River, was established. In 1900 the Chicago Sanitary and Ship Canal was opened, reversing the flow of the Chicago River and carrying the industrial and domestic wastes of Chicago into the Mississippi River. This canal was enlarged in 1933 to permit navigation.

Railroads and highways parallel the river and canals, taking advantage of the Des Plaines valley into Chicago.

Petroleum tanks and a fuel power plant are located adjacent to the canal, receiving their supplies from barges. Petroleum products and coal are the principal cargoes transported on the canal. An oil refinery is located along the canal.

1. Why are the wastes of Chicago discharged into the Mississippi River and not into Lake Michigan? Find out what laws govern Chicago's use of Lake Michigan water.
2. What products are transported on the canal? What indicates the nature of the cargoes on the map and aerial photograph?
3. What products do the road and railroad carry?
4. Explain the origin of the spoil banks along the Chicago Sanitary and Ship Canal.

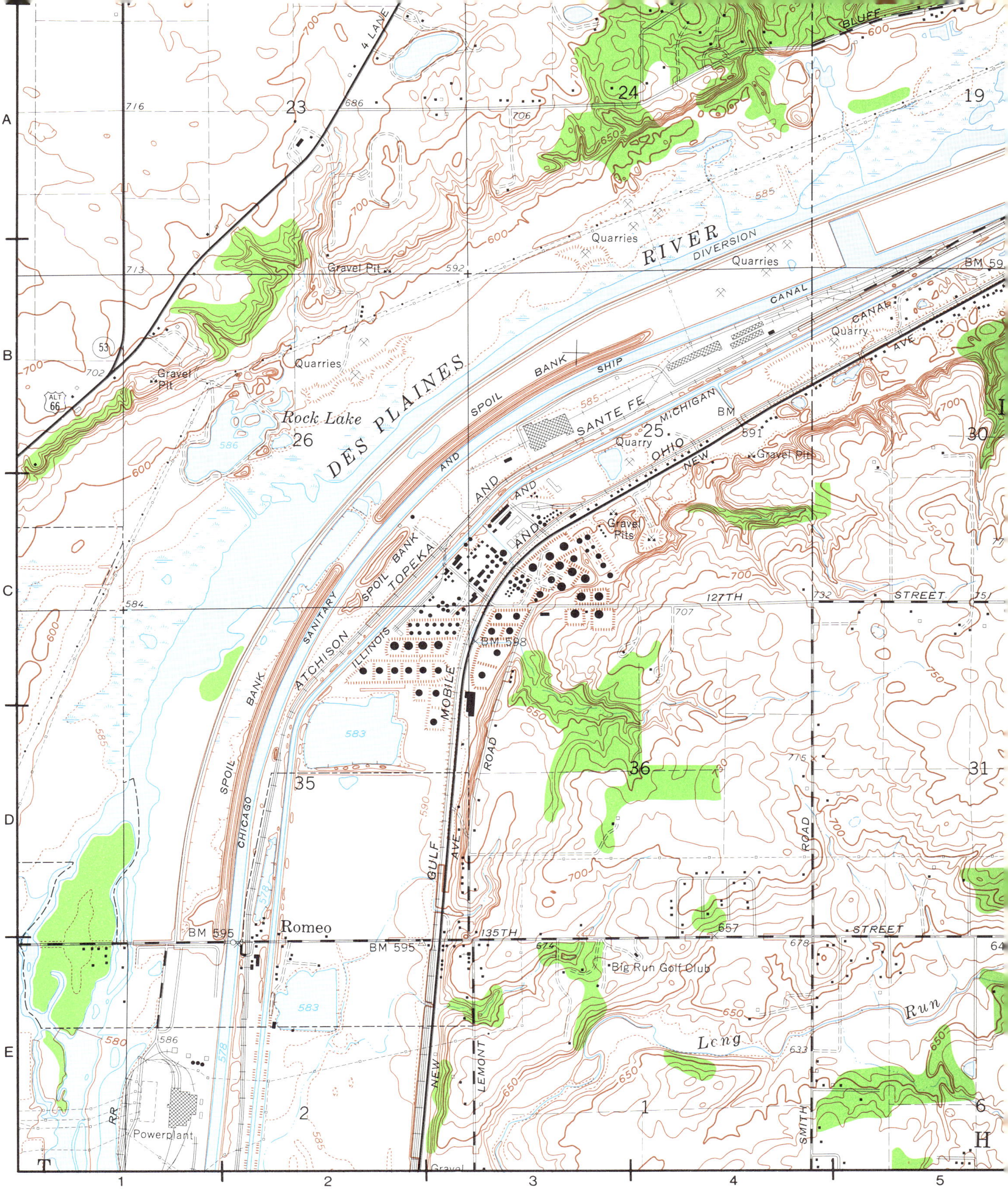

from Romeoville Quadrangle, Illinois

Scale 1:24,000
Contour Interval 10 ft.
Latitude 41° 38′ N
to 41° 41′ N
Longitude 88° 01′ W
to 88° 04′ 30″ W

Urban Impressions

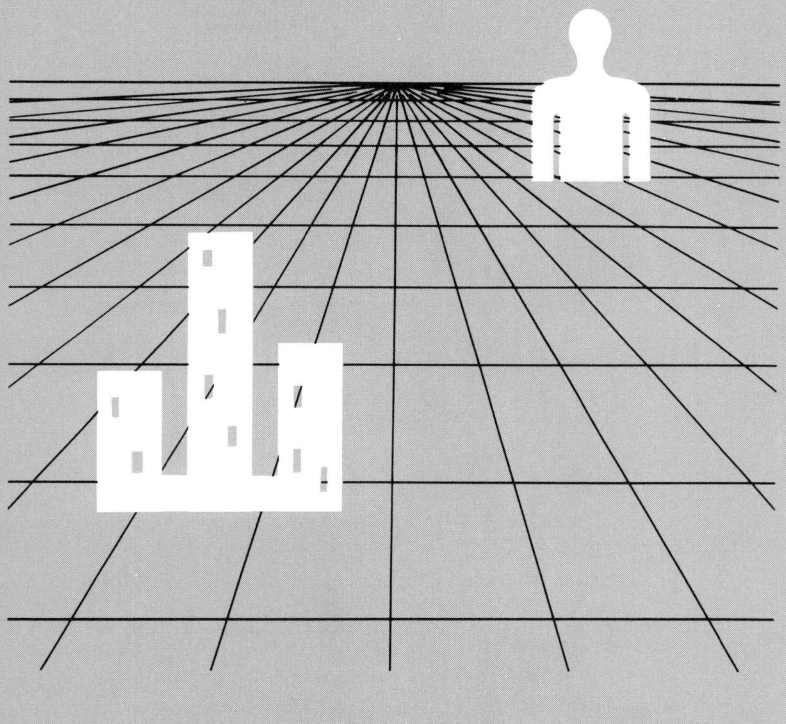

As compared to only 5 percent in 1790, over 70 percent of the population of the United States now lives in cities that occupy only about 0.2 percent of the land. By the year 2000, about 90 percent of the population will be living in cities. Therefore, urban population density is very high. The density per square mile in New York City is almost 26,000 and in Chicago about 17,000.

Some of the earliest cities grew along the Atlantic Coast, where harbor facilities were available. They relied on the production and demands of their hinterlands for economic growth. The flow of goods between producing regions and ports often required a change in the mode or direction of transportation, and numerous cities grew at the "break-of-bulk" points where the transfer of goods took place.

The first industrial cities were established where water power was available, but with the development of heavy industry proximity to coalfields and iron mines became an important factor. Other cities developed around forts, universities, government activities and recreation sites.

A modern phenomenon of urban growth is the suburb. Its inhabitants are those who have moved away from the congestion of the central city and commute daily to their places of work in the city.

The city is indicated on these topographic maps in gray. Various functional features, such as railroads, freeways, the central business district and principal buildings such as schools, churches, government buildings, museums and hospitals, may be identified within the gray tint. The central business district occupies the heart of the city and includes stores and services.

The central business district is surrounded by wholesale and manufacturing districts, the buildings of which appear as black or gray symbols. Numerous water tanks, oil or gas tanks and railroad yards are usually present. Where water transport is available, docks, slips, general cargo sheds, elevators, cranes, bridges, navigation lights and channel markers may be seen. On the aerial photograph, the wholesale and manufacturing districts appear as agglomerations of sprawling structures with chimneys, monitor roofs, roof ventilators, power lines and railroad tracks.

Beyond the manufacturing area is the residential area. High-rise apartments give way to smaller apartments and finally to individual residences toward the periphery of the city. Older residential sections may be identified by regularly spaced streets that conform to the original city plan and the presence of numerous schools, churches, and parks. When viewed on the aerial photograph, the houses and streets in older residential areas are partially obscured by large trees.

The new residential areas lie along the periphery of the city or in the suburbs. The map may show individual houses on winding streets, many of which are dead end streets or cul-de-sacs. Suburban structures sprawl over large areas around the central city. As the city grows in prosperity, its suburbs grow outward, taking over the surrounding countryside. Eventually, they may merge with the suburbs of a neighboring city, forming a continuous urban complex. New York City and many cities of New Jersey, New York and Connecticut have grown together in this manner to form a "megalopolis."

CHARLESTON, SOUTH CAROLINA

Charleston is the site of one of the early seventeenth century settlements along the Atlantic coast of the United States which became a leading twentieth century metropolitan area and important port. In the early 1670's colonists from England and Barbados landed on the west bank of the Ashley River at Albemarle Point. This low and marshy site was not only infested with malaria but also difficult to defend. As a result, the colony was moved to Oyster Point on the east bank of the river in 1680.

In 1674 rice cultivation was introduced. The crop improved the economy of the colony, but it tied the population to the lowlands and did little to alleviate the malaria. By 1700, rice production had increased to the extent that there were not enough ships to export it. Rice was subsequently replaced by indigo and following the War of 1812, long staple, Sea Island cotton became important.

In the latter part of the eighteenth century Charleston was incorporated, and since then it has flourished economically. The harbor facilities were developed toward the end of the nineteenth century and in the early twentieth century. Features such as the dry docks, cargo sheds, U.S. Customs House, and U.S. Coast Guard Station indicate the importance of Charleston as a port.

The streets of Charleston do not form the regular rectangular pattern, typical of so many American cities. They follow old plat boundaries and are oriented to the peninsular location of the city. King Street marks the location of the King's Highway, which reached Charleston in 1738.

Today, Charleston is a major seaport on the Atlantic coast. Its industries include oil refineries, pulp and paper mills and fertilizer plants.

1. Describe the street pattern of Charleston.
2. What evidence is there on the map and photograph that Charleston is an educational center?
3. What are the major differences between Charleston, South Carolina, and Stickney, shown on Berwyn, Illinois, quadrangle?
4. Where is the major industrial area of Charleston located? List the industrial features which can be identified there.
5. Why is a sunken ship indicated on the map?
6. Why are petroleum storage tanks placed in revetments?
7. Where is the central business district located? Explain reasons for your answer.

from Charleston Quadrangle, South Carolina

½ 0 1 MILE

1 .5 0 1 KILOMETER

Scale 1:24,000
Contour Interval 5 ft.
Latitude 32° 46′ N to 32° 49′ N
Longitude 79° 55′ W to 79° 58′ W

FOND DU LAC, WISCONSIN

Fond du Lac, as its name implies, is located at the "foot of the lake." It was established on Lake Winnebago in 1785 as a trading post by French trappers and explorers. Shortly after 1850, impetus was given to the growth of Fond du Lac by the lumbering industry. As lumbering gained importance in the surrounding forests, logs were floated on the Wolf River and Lake Winnebago to the saw mills and wood-processing plants in Fond du Lac. By 1880, however, the industry had moved farther north making it unprofitable to ship logs all the way to Fond du Lac. Today, the industry that remains is located along Fond du Lac River or to the north of the city.

Because of its location on Lake Winnebago and in a lowland, numerous transportation routes converged at Fond du Lac. U.S. 151 follows the route of the old Military Road which was built in 1835 from Green Bay to Portage (by way of Fond du Lac), and on to Prairie du Chien on the Mississippi River. In 1859 the Chicago and Northwestern Railroad connected the city to Chicago.

Although it is a small city, many representative urban features, such as a sewage treatment plant, radio tower, railroad tracks, freight yards and railroad shop can be observed. The attraction of a water body for recreation and aesthetic values is implied by the number of dwellings that are located along the shoreline, giving rise to a line settlement pattern.

1. Name some features that indicate the importance of tourism in and around Fond du Lac.
2. Describe land use along the shoreline. Compare it with lake-shore land use at Superior, Wisconsin. At Gary, Indiana.
3. Was the city built before or after the completion of the Public Land Survey in the region?
4. What are the major forms of transportation that serve the region?
5. Compare the photographs of Fond du Lac and Charleston with those of Gary, Indiana, and Berwyn, Illinois. How do small towns differ from industrial cities?
6. Compare the patterns of the new residential subdivisions in Fond du Lac with those on the Cumberland, Maryland, and Ventura, California, quadrangles. Explain what you observe.

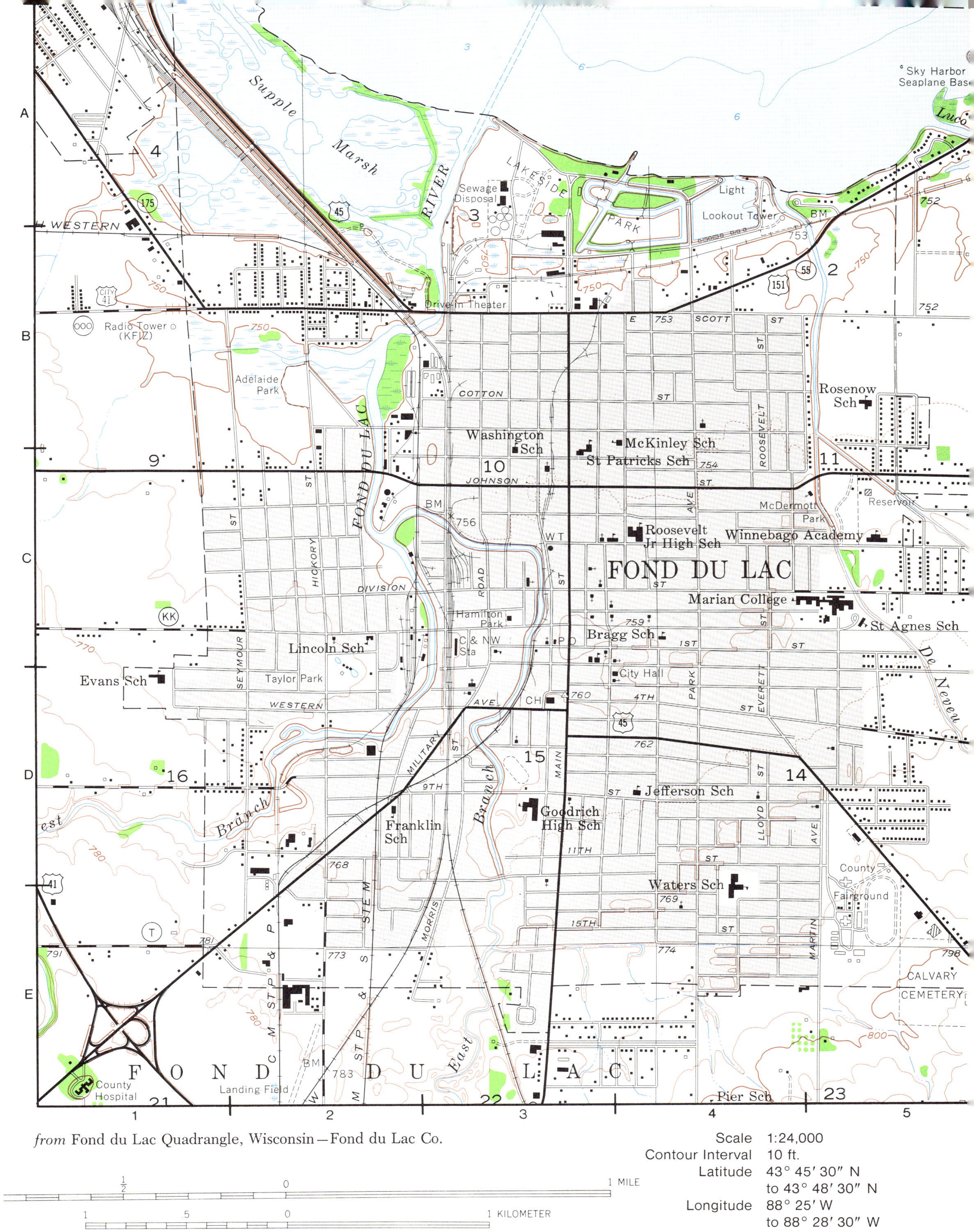

from Fond du Lac Quadrangle, Wisconsin—Fond du Lac Co.

Scale 1:24,000
Contour Interval 10 ft.
Latitude 43° 45′ 30″ N to 43° 48′ 30″ N
Longitude 88° 25′ W to 88° 28′ 30″ W

VENTURA, CALIFORNIA

The original settlement on the site of Ventura, California, was a Franciscan mission called San Buenaventura. It was founded by Father Junipero Serra in 1782. When the mission was established, Father Serra consecrated the land north of the mission and marked it with a cross. This land is now occupied by Grant Park.

The city of Ventura occupies the narrow coastal plain and the valley of the Ventura River. New residential subdivisions, however, spread upward on the hillsides. In the vicinity of Ventura Junior College, some of the homes are more than 250 feet above the urbanized area, providing the occupants with an excellent view of the coastal plain and sea shore.

The city serves a large citrus fruit-growing area where lemons and oranges are grown. Another product of the region is petroleum, which is extracted in the hills to the north of the city. The oil is transported by underground pipe to Pierpont Bay where it is loaded into oil tankers.

Recreation features can be identified in the area. A state beach is maintained along Pierpont Bay, along with a baseball park and county fairgrounds. All major transportation routes are confined to the narrow coastal area and the river valleys.

1. What factors control the shape of the city?
2. Describe the land use along the shoreline.
3. What factors influence the street pattern in Ventura?
4. Compare this town of Spanish origin with Abiquiu, New Mexico, which is also of Spanish origin. Give reasons for the differences.
5. Both Charleston, South Carolina, and Ventura attract tourists. What types of attractions does each offer?
6. Compare the shapes of buildings in Ventura with those in Charleston, South Carolina. Explain the differences.
7. Describe the vegetation in this area. How is it influenced by climate and slope?

from Ventura Quadrangle, California—Ventura Co.

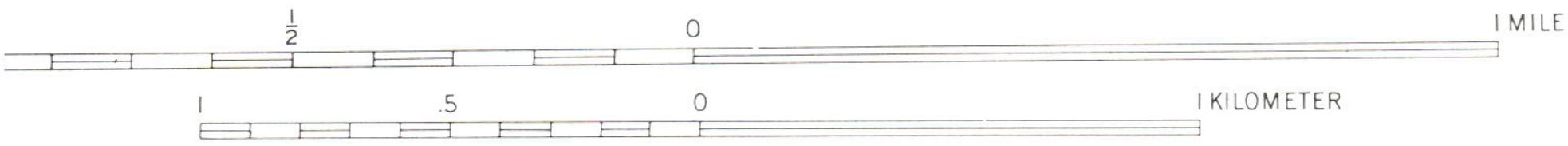

Scale 1:24,000
Contour Interval 20 ft.
Latitude 34° 15′ N to 34° 18′ N
Longitude 119° 15′ W to 119° 18′ W

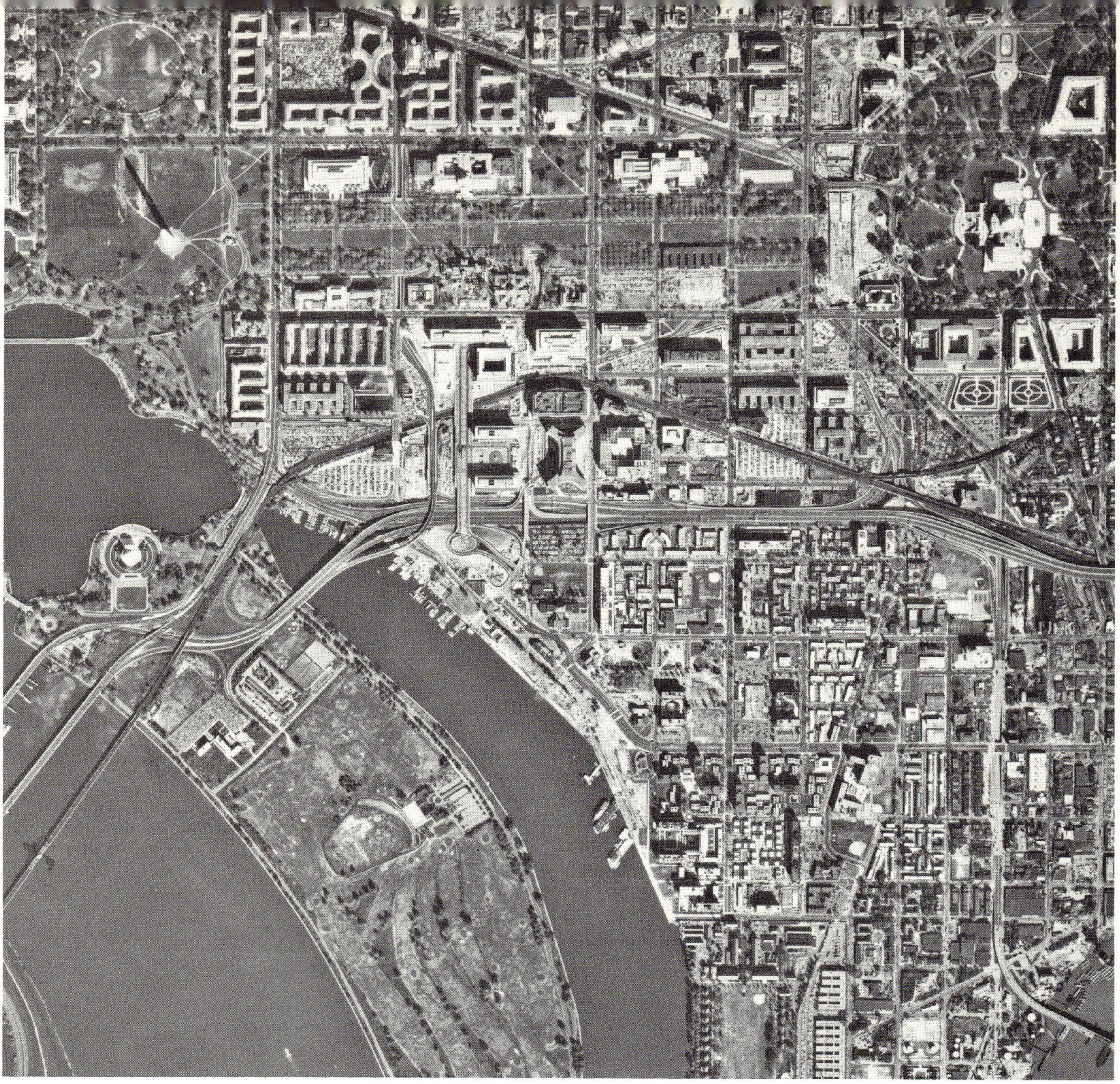

WASHINGTON WEST, DISTRICT OF COLUMBIA/MARYLAND/VIRGINIA

Washington, D.C., is a planned city, the function of which is almost entirely confined to government activities. It is located on the Potomac River at the Fall Line between the Atlantic Coastal Plain and the Appalachian Piedmont. Before the city developed, the Potomac Valley had a swampy bottom and rising in a series of Pleistocene terraces.

The city has a distinctive radial pattern of major streets that radiate from points of importance. Underlying this pattern is the typical rectangular pattern of minor streets. This design was created by the city planner, Pierre Charles l'Enfant. With the development of technology, many of the marshes were drained and are now occupied by modern buildings.

The area along the Potomac Parkway is called Foggy Bottom. This area of high-rise apartments was formerly a low, damp swampy area in which were located the houses of workers, the brewery and the gashouse. The area to the west of Rock Creek lies on the Piedmont and includes upper class residences and foreign embassies. The downtown area of Washington begins north of the government office buildings.

1. What are the advantages of a radial street pattern?
2. Identify some of the landmarks of Washington, D.C. on the map. Locate them on the aerial photograph.
3. Examine the contour pattern of Capitol Hill. What is the origin of this landform?
4. Where are most of the government buildings located?
5. What did the land around the Potomac Parkway and the Washington Monument look like two hundred years ago?
6. Washington, D.C., is located on the Fall Line. What is the Fall Line and what physiographic regions does it separate? Locate evidences on the Fall Line on the aerial photograph.

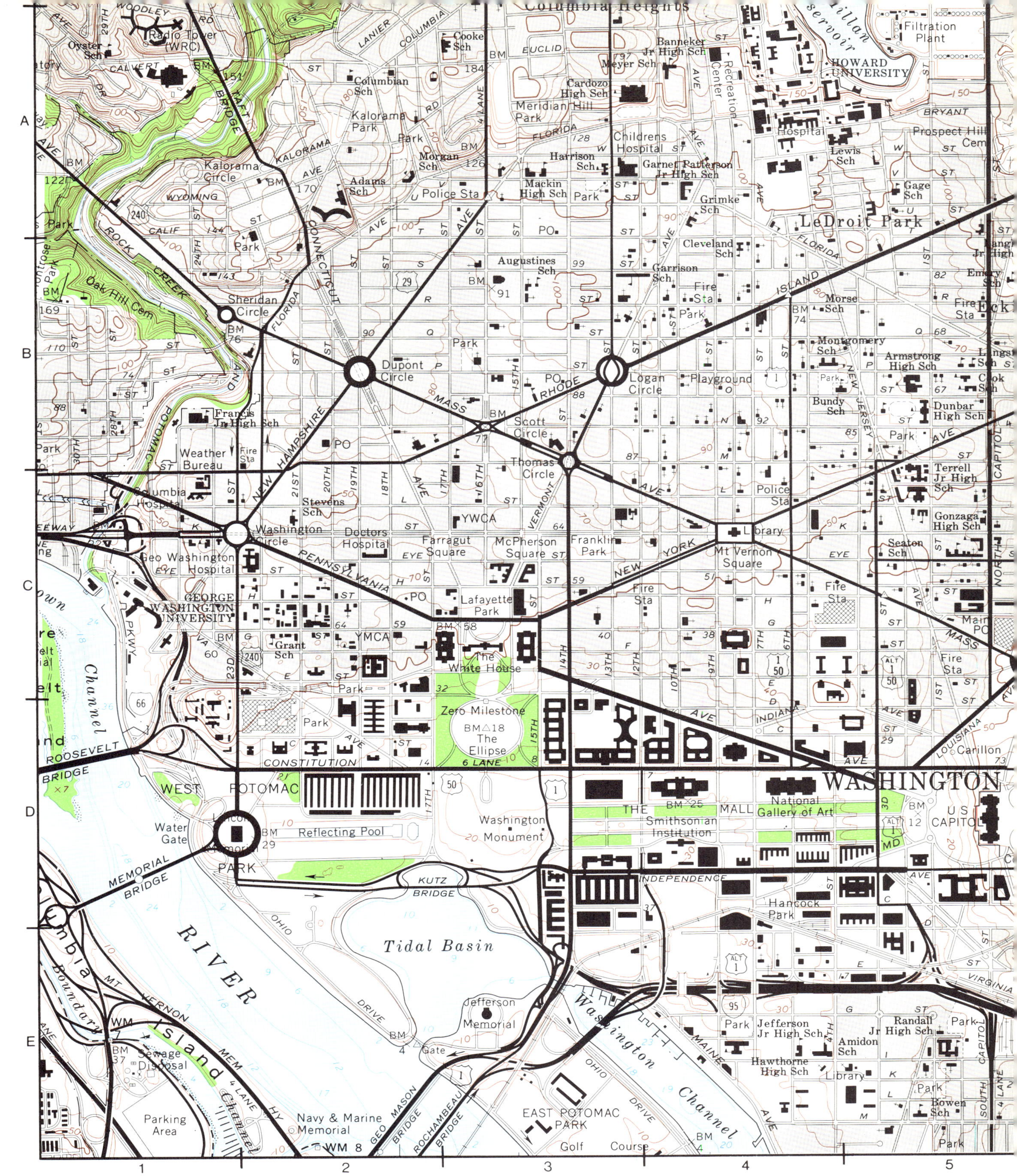

from Washington West Quadrangle, District of Columbia/Maryland/Virginia

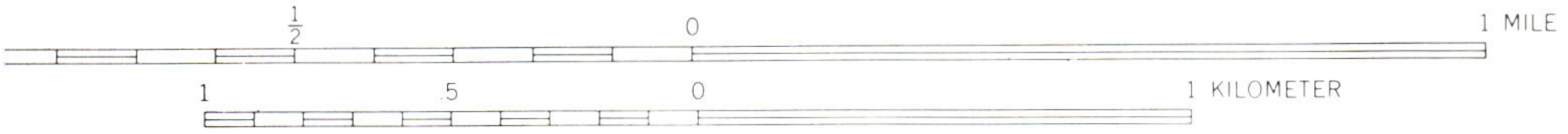

Scale 1:24,000
Contour Interval 10 ft.
Latitude 38° 52′ 30″ N to 38° 55′ 30″ N
Longitude 77° 01′ W to 77° 04′ W

NORTH KANSAS CITY, MISSOURI/KANSAS

Kansas City is located at the confluence of the Missouri and Kansas rivers. The original settlement on this site was Westport. It was located at the head of navigation on the Missouri River, and was the starting point of the Oregon and Santa Fe trails. It served as an outfitting post for overland pioneering expeditions to the west. When the railroad came to this region, the first railroad bridge to span the Missouri River was built at Westport. The name of the city was changed to Kansas City in 1889.

Kansas City soon became the main supplier of meat to the surrounding army posts, railroad construction camps and other settlements, and extensive stockyards and meat-packing works were organized. Today Kansas City has numerous industries and has become a major railroad center. The map and photograph show the industrial complex in the northern part of the city. The industrial sections of the city are confined to the river but the business and residential areas have expanded on the bluffs that border the valley.

1. Where is Kansas City, Kansas, located with respect to Kansas City, Missouri?
2. What indications of river control works appear on the map? On the aerial photograph?
3. Explain the location of the industrial areas. Account for the location of the tank farm.
4. Explain the locations of the two airports seen on this map. What sites do they occupy? Compare the locations of these airports with the one on the Berwyn quadrangle.

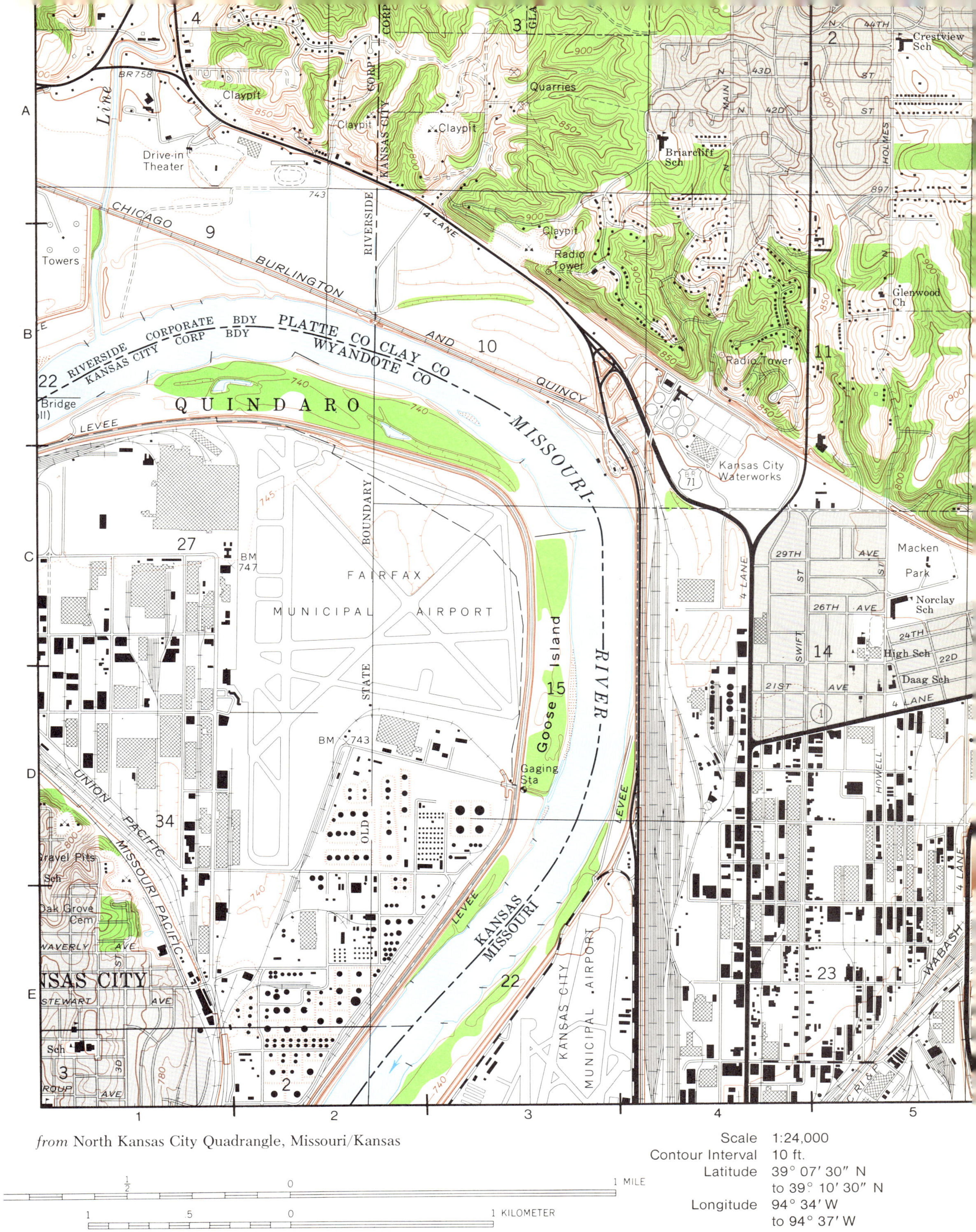

from North Kansas City Quadrangle, Missouri/Kansas

Scale 1:24,000
Contour Interval 10 ft.
Latitude 39° 07′ 30″ N to 39° 10′ 30″ N
Longitude 94° 34′ W to 94° 37′ W

PITTSBURGH WEST, PENNSYLVANIA

Pittsburgh became an important city because of its strategic location and accessibility to natural resources. Located at the confluence of the Monongahela and Allegheny rivers, where the Ohio River is formed, the Forks of the Ohio became hotly contested by both the English and French in the middle of the eighteenth century. William Penn laid claim to the area in 1681, and La Salle proclaimed all lands drained by the Mississippi River and its tributaries (including this area) under French control in 1682.

Finally, in 1754, the British began construction of a small fort; but before it was completed, the fort was seized by the French. It was completed later and named Fort Duquesne. The French abandoned it in 1758, when the British occupied it again.

Numerous roads were built connecting the forks of the Ohio to the Atlantic, and settlers began to pour into the region. Pittsburgh, at the forks of the Ohio, was the principal outfitting point for migration down the Ohio River.

Coal and iron were discovered in the surrounding areas and industrial Pittsburgh began to take shape. By 1859 it had become an important manufacturing city.

1. Pittsburgh is a major industrial city like Gary, Indiana. Do the two cities resemble each other? Explain your answer.
2. How has the growth pattern of Pittsburgh been influenced by topography?
3. What was the first major route to Pittsburgh from the east?
4. Is the street pattern always rectangular? Why? What is the rectangular pattern influenced by?
5. What are the major differences between the urban areas north and south of the rivers?
6. Give evidences of the large amount of traffic that crosses the rivers.
7. What type of industry is located on Brunot Island?

from Pittsburgh West Quadrangle, Pennsylvania—Allegheny Co.

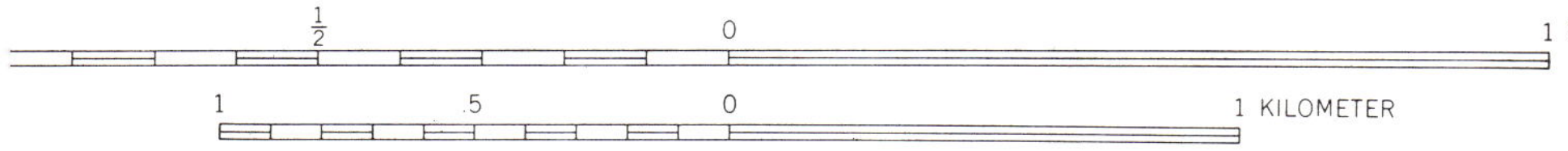

Scale	1:24,000
Contour Interval	20 ft.
Latitude	40° 25′ N to 40° 28′ N
Longitude	80° W to 80° 03′ 30″ W

BERWYN, ILLINOIS (Stickney)

The urban development in the map shows Stickney, a southwestern suburb of Chicago, along with a part of Chicago itself to the south. Stickney is not a typical American suburb with numerous, widely spaced homes on large, grassy lots and some modern, clean industrial plants. The region is a part of the giant industrial development of south and southwest Chicago. Until about 1850, this densely settled region was occupied by a series of swampy ridges and troughs which were the remains of the ancient glacial Lake Chicago. When the swamps were drained, settlement began; today it is one of the most densely populated regions of the United States.

Because of its location on the major transportation routes and on the periphery of the industrial district, this area has developed into an important distribution center. Signs of the complex transportation facilities are apparent. The Chicago Sanitary and Ship Canal and the Illinois and Michigan Canal provide navigable waterways for heavy bulk goods. These canals, together with the Des Plaines River, connect Chicago to the Mississippi River, thus providing a continuous waterway from Chicago to the Gulf of Mexico. The water transport facilities are supplemented by a complex railroad network and its associated warehouses, marshalling yards and maze of railroad tracks.

1. Name some features that indicate the heavy industrialization of the region. Where are they located?
2. Describe the different modes of transportation in the area.
3. What form of transportation does the Clearing Industrial District rely on?
4. Examine the airfield partially visible in the eastern part of the map. Does it appear to be large enough for a giant metropolitan area like Chicago? Explain.
5. Compare the photograph with that of Gary, Indiana. What are the similarities? Differences?

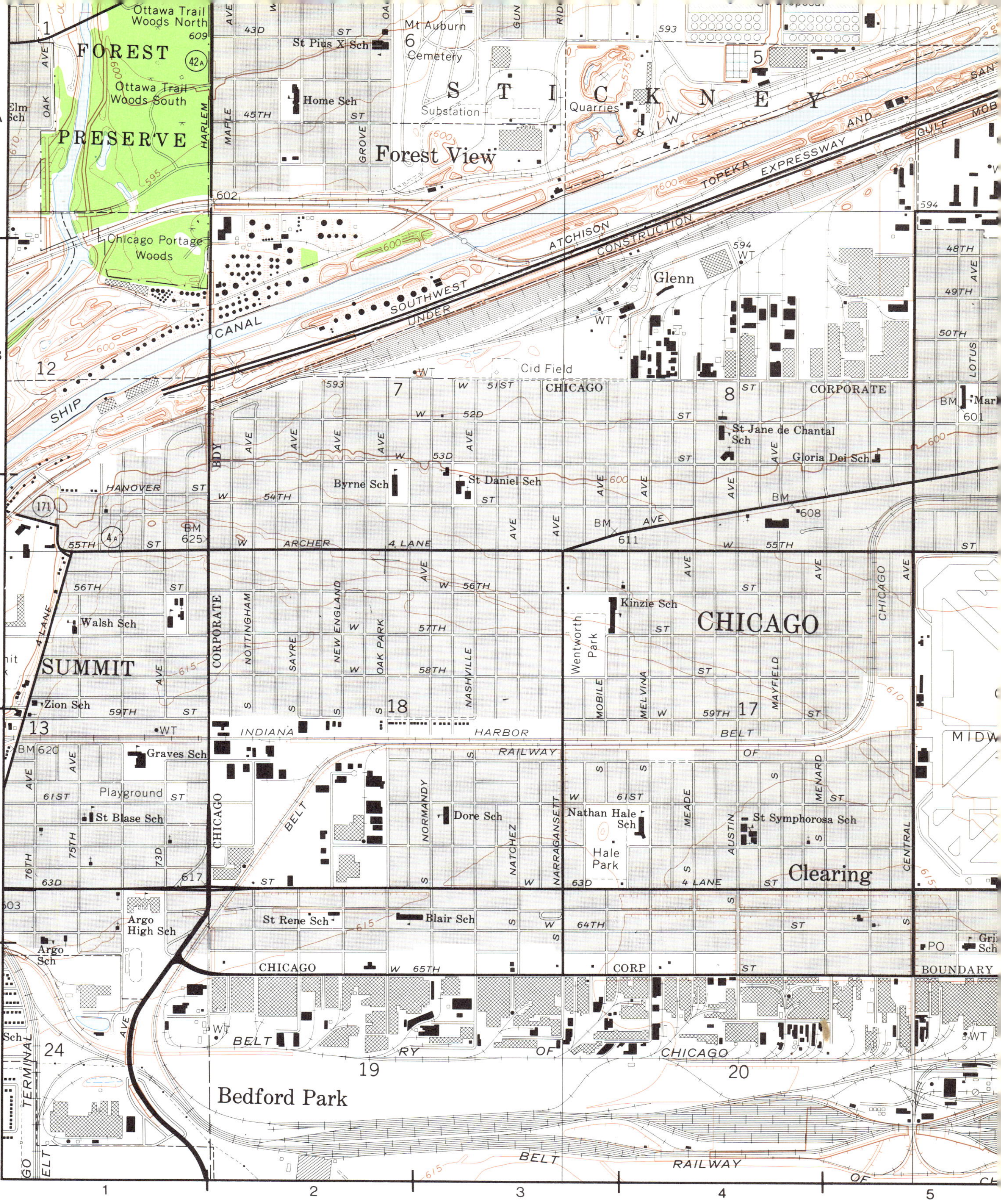

from Berwyn Quadrangle, Illinois—Cook Co.

½ 0 1 MILE

1 .5 0 1 KILOMETER

Scale 1:24,000
Contour Interval 5 ft.
Latitude 41° 46′ N
to 41° 49′ N
Longitude 87° 45′ 30″ W
to 87° 48′ 30″ W

Index to cultural features by map

In this index, the cultural features are listed alphabetically under the title of the map. The index is arranged alphabetically by states. To locate specific cultural features when the map is not known, see the alphabetical index, beginning on page 94.

Alphabetical index